unanticipated — has Dooley published ~~exhaustive~~ (?) command of JMC: competent but directionless — doesn't guide

string of ?_____

double check in intro,

No CONCLUSION!

yes, back cover blurb suggests so!

need more biog. info

also 1° reading
poor use of 2° readings, see 5] ~ no 9] — uses chunks of ~~text~~ to prove point / conclude points, w/o organising
pedestrian, chronological approach

disorganised / loosely organised survey of key themes in (Coetzee's) work.

signals some possible new directions enquiry (ₐ this in Boyhood + Waiting, intro)

→ use C. on language as example — broad, slightly drastic switches, jumps from Coetzee's ?rightful sensibility (118) to music as lang. to Benchtiman (?) writing of novels ?such ?as glossa to naming.

↓
connxn w C. on point of view could be exploited here.

GW01425154

J.M. Coetzee

AND THE

Power of Narrative

J.M. Coetzee

AND THE
Power of Narrative

GILLIAN DOOLEY

CAMBRIA PRESS

Amherst, New York

Requests for permission should be directed to:
permissions@cambriapress.com, or mailed to:
Cambria Press
20 Northpointe Parkway, Suite 188
Amherst, NY 14228

The author thanks the Australian Book Review for permission to reproduce
material in chapter 2 of this book.

Library of Congress Cataloging-in-Publication Data

Dooley, Gillian, 1955-
    J. M. Coetzee and the power of narrative / Gillian Dooley.
       p. cm.
    Includes bibliographical references and index.
    ISBN 978-1-60497-673-1 (alk. paper)
 1. Coetzee, J. M., 1940—Criticism and interpretation. I. Title.

    PR9369.3.C58Z639 2010
    823'.914—dc22

2009051868

TABLE OF CONTENTS

ACKNOWLEDGMENTS

I am grateful to generous friends and colleagues who have read all or part of this book and made suggestions. In particular, I would like to thank Sue Sheridan, Robert Phiddian, and Debra Zott. For more general moral support, I would like to acknowledge Joost Daalder, Aliese Millington, Graham Tulloch, and Robert Lumsden.

Adele Lenz and Ralph Shlomowitz were both helpful with questions regarding the South African background of Coetzee's work.

Thanks are also due to all at Cambria Press who have made it such an easy and pleasant experience to produce this book.

I also thank J. M. Coetzee for his gracious permission to quote from his works, where the extracts quoted exceed the fair use provisions of copyright legislation.

LIST OF ABBREVIATIONS

AI	*Age of Iron*
B	*Boyhood*
D	*Disgrace*
DBY	*Diary of a Bad Year*
DL	*Dusklands*
DP	*Doubling the Point*
EC	*Elizabeth Costello*
F	*Foe*
HC	*From the Heart of the Country*
MK	*Life & Times of Michael K*
MP	*Master of Petersburg*
S	*Summertime*
SM	*Slow Man*
SS	*Stranger Shores*
WB	*Waiting for the Barbarians*
Y	*Youth*

I don't attach quite the same significance to demystification as an animating principle of criticism as the left does or did. That is, I no longer see opening up the mystifications in which ordinary life is wrapped as a necessary aim, or indeed an obligation, of criticism. ... A healthy level of suspiciousness is not a bad thing. But some of my criticism...is soured, I think, by a certain relentless suspiciousness of appearances. Why am I now suspicious of such suspiciousness? For two reasons. First, in the act of triumphantly tearing the clothes off its subject and displaying the nakedness beneath—"Behold the truth!"—it exposes a naïveté of its own. For is the naked body really the truth? And second, because a critical practice whose climactic gesture is always a triumphant tearing-off, as it grows lazy (and every orthodoxy grows lazy) begins to confine its attentions to clothed subjects, and even to subjects whose clothes are easily torn off. In other words...a demystifying criticism privileges mystifications. It becomes like Quixote scouring the plains for giants to tilt at, and ignoring everything but windmills.

—J. M. Coetzee, *Doubling the Point* 106

J.M. Coetzee

AND THE

Power of Narrative

CHAPTER 1

INTRODUCTION

My intention in writing about J. M. Coetzee's work is perhaps most easily defined by negatives. Much excellent criticism of Coetzee—and, it might be said, some less-than-excellent criticism as well—puts his work in context: historical, political, literary, and theoretical. Laura Wright, in the introduction to her book *Writing "Out of All the Camps,"* gives a useful summary of the political and historical dimension of his work. Dominic Head's *Cambridge Introduction to J. M. Coetzee* is particularly good on the links between Coetzee's ideas and his creative work. David Attwell's book *J. M. Coetzee: South Africa and the Politics of Writing* explores literary, historical, and political contexts with subtlety and sophistication. Michela Cancpari-Labib in *Old Myths, Modern Empires* concentrates on explicating literary and theoretical "intertexts" to Coetzee's novels. A myriad of other critics have discussed the work in relation to the major literary theorists and in their South African context.

However, it was not until I read Derek Attridge's *J. M. Coetzee and the Ethics of Reading* and his other essays on Coetzee that I found a critic with whom I felt I shared an interest in trying to understand how Coetzee uses narrative form and how the reader experiences the text, rather than regarding it as "an object whose significance has to be divined" (Attridge, "Against Allegory" 67). One is caught by something unique and valuable in art, and one feels the urge to explain its effects. It is all too easy to become caught up in explication of what the artist means to say, though this often misses the point and fails to account for one's experience of the work. As Attridge points out in his discussion of *Waiting for the Barbarians*,

> Once we attend to the details of our encounter with the novel, these seem far in excess of the allegorizations we are tempted to produce—and more explanatory of our enjoying and prizing of the novel than the political, historical, or moral truths that we can apprehend perfectly well without Coetzee's aid. ("Against Allegory" 71)

Coetzee's novels are often described as "novels of ideas" because of their undeniable intellectual force. However, the ideas in his novels are, significantly, always embodied and tested up to and beyond their limits in a suffering, mortal being, and the language and narrative forms in which they are expressed are constantly interrogated.

So, I am not interested in examining the "what" or even the "why" of Coetzee's work in any detail, although such questions inevitably arise from time to time in the following pages. I want to discover the "how": whence does Coetzee's work derive its power? A discussion of themes, influences, and allegorical meanings, it seems to me, tends to bleach out the experience of reading, and this experience is surely the reason for choosing to read Coetzee. An allegorical or thematic reading often ignores style, language, point of view, and narrative structure. Sometimes linguistic analysis can be brought to the service of such a reading. John Douthwaite's articles on *Disgrace*, for example, provide some interesting insights into Coetzee's use of language, choice of names, and so on, although this approach can lead to some dubious interpretations when taken too literally.

I am also not concerned to any great degree in this book with questions of influence, either generally or in specific cases where books are clearly based on the works of earlier writers—Defoe, Dostoevsky, Kafka, and so on. I tend to agree with Nadine Gordimer when she writes, "I would…raise an eyebrow at, if not take issue with, critical contention that the difficulties of Coetzee's novels require that the reader shall have read the same books the author has" (Preface x–xi). Once again, a catalogue of intertexts says nothing about Coetzee's power and value as a writer.

Writing about a writer with Coetzee's ferocious intellect and breadth of reference is daunting. When novelist Paul Auster, speaking at Writers' Week in Adelaide in 2008, remarked that he is stimulated to write about things he does not understand, I felt this explained my wish to write about Coetzee. His books are endlessly fascinating because they are not finally explicable: a residue of mystery remains. It is for this reason that much of my criticism is tentative and open-ended. Dominic Head notes how Coetzee's novels

> wilfully resist any critical attempt to master or reduce. This means that the element of misrepresentation that is evident in all criticism is, perhaps, highlighted most especially in criticism of Coetzee's novels. And this may sound like a particular hostage to fortune at the beginning of an introductory volume of this kind; but it does give me the opportunity to place stress on the need for openness in the reading of a novel by Coetzee, even while acknowledging the difficulty of sustaining that openness. (*Cambridge* xi)

I read this passage just as I was preparing my final draft of this book and found it heartening. As Attridge says, "If Coetzee's novels and memoirs exemplify anything, it is the value (but also the risk) of openness to the moment and to the future, of the perhaps and the wherever" ("Against Allegory" 79). The kind of reading both Attridge and Head recommend brings the focus back to the text and cannot be separated from it.

The power of narrative to grip the reader's attention and wrench one away from the demands of everyday life has little to do with political messages or literary influences. This question of the power of the writer is one that Coetzee revisits often and has perhaps not entirely resolved in his own mind. He has consistently resisted requests to interpret his own work. His discomfort at being thought a powerful writer was evident in his interview with Tony Morphet in 1987: "'Successful author' is a barbed phrase, here, a highly barbed phrase. ... In this interview, I am being installed in a position of power—power, in this case, over my own text" (Morphet 462). *Foe* and *Master of Petersburg* engage quite directly with the dangers of authorial power; *Slow Man* and *Diary of a Bad Year*, perhaps, deal more with its limits: the writing personae in the later novels, although eminent, have not achieved the pinnacle of success and recognition in the same way Coetzee has. But the kind of power that I have in mind is not the power that an author arrogates to himself, but the power that emanates from writing like Coetzee's. The strength and force of his vision compels the reader to face squarely whatever he presents, however appalling, knowing that the writer is also appalled but that he has nevertheless resisted the temptation to avert his eyes or to find consolation in ideology or theory.

In the following seven chapters, I have tried several approaches to Coetzee's narratives. Chapter 2 examines the type of resistance to be found in his work, a resistance which seems to have little basis in a political belief or a rational philosophy of justice. I chart the evolution of Coetzee's public position on politics and writing and look at how his reluctance to claim power or to place trust in political solutions has been manifested in his books. In chapter 3, I trace the effects of Coetzee's choice of point of view in each of his books: how it interacts with questions of complicity and impressions of realism, how it relates to the subject matter and characters he is dealing with in each case. I consider aspects like the sex of the various narrators and the level of identification which is possible between Coetzee and his alter egos, as well as the simple distinction between first- and third-person narrators and the rhetorical position of each book.

Chapter 4 is an exploration of the place of the comic arts in Coetzee's work. This is a subject which has routinely been dismissed by critics who have failed to discern any humor in the novels. My contention is that a sense of the ridiculous and absurd is implicit in much of Coetzee's narrative prose and can be seen in the underlying structure of all his books.

Chapter 5 concerns his use of language and languages: the choice of tenses, the surprising flights of imagery to be found amidst the taut elegance of his narrative style, and also the multilingual sensibilities he shares with many of his characters, not excluding the nonverbal language of music.

In the next two chapters, I follow a thematic approach. The subject of sex and desire has, it seems to me, attracted less critical attention than various other themes, and, of those critics who have considered it, most seem bent on extracting allegories of sexual politics, for example from *Disgrace*, which are not necessarily warranted by a close examination of the texts. In chapter 6, I dispute some of these readings and suggest some other ways of considering the subject. Chapter 7 looks at another uncomfortable aspect of Coetzee's books: his treatment of the bond between parents and children. Children can be significant as either presences or absences in the novels; parents or parent figures are often rivals or oppressors. Childhood itself has many shades of meaning, in memory or imagination, and real children often fail to fulfill the roles projected by hopeful adults, despite their potency as symbols of the future.

In the last chapter, I turn my attention to the endings of Coetzee's narratives in the belief that the endings inevitably color all that comes before. My aim is to see how the choice of conclusion—time, place, point of view—contributes to the possible meanings and impressions left by each book. Many of these endings are enigmatic and resist interpretation: the end of *Disgrace* is particularly puzzling and has provoked some ingenious critical attempts at explication. Again, my hope is to see not what these endings signify but how they operate to project the reader's attention back to the rest of the book.

Rita Barnard warns, when discussing the final scene of *Disgrace*, that "it is essential that we do not, as it were, try to beat it into convenient shape with a critical shovel" (223). The temptation of wielding a critical shovel, or "of triumphantly tearing the clothes off its subject and displaying the nakedness beneath" (*DP* 106), is inimical to the subtleties of Coetzee's art. When I have failed to resist this temptation, I hope I have been tentative enough to be spared from accusations of violence and triumphalism.

Jolly

CHAPTER 2

COETZEE'S FREEDOM

In the 1980s, when it seemed that the situation in South Africa would never improve, debate raged about the responsibility of South African novelists to act as witnesses to and opponents of apartheid. Some believed that white writers, especially, should use their privileged position in the fight. Nadine Gordimer was prominent among those who felt it was essential to be, in J. M. Coetzee's words, a "stripper-away of convenient illusions and unmasker of colonial bad faith" ("Awakening" 7) in the realist convention, rather than a spinner of postmodern metafictions.

Gordimer, born in 1923, was by then already a major figure on the world literary scene. Her first book was published in 1949, and by 1980, she had produced seven novels and nine volumes of short stories. She had won the Booker Prize in 1974 for *The Conservationist*. Coetzee, born in 1940, was a relative newcomer. His first novel, *Dusklands*, was published in 1974, and his first Booker win came in 1983 for his fourth, *Life & Times of Michael K.* Reviewing the novel in the *New York Review*, Gordimer complained that "while it is implicitly and highly

political, Coetzee's heroes are those who ignore history, not make it."
She went on:

> [T]his is a challengingly questionable position for a writer to take
> up in South Africa, make no mistake about it. The presentation of
> the truth and meaning of what white has done to black stands out
> on every page, celebrating its writer's superb, unafraid creative
> energy as it does; yet it denies the energy of the will to resist evil.
> That *this* superb energy exists with indefatigable and undefeatable
> persistence among the black people of South Africa—Michael
> K's people—is made evident, yes, heroically, every grinding day.
> It is not present in the novel. ...
>
> A revulsion against all political and revolutionary solutions
> rises with the insistence of the song of cicadas to the climax of
> this novel.
>
> I don't think the author would deny that it is his own revul-
> sion. ... The organicism that George Lukács defines as the inte-
> gral relation between private and social destiny is distorted here
> more than is allowed for by the subjectivity that is in every writer.
> ("Idea" 6)

Coetzee is not combative. He seems not to enjoy arguing and prefers to
leave interpretation of his work to others. He told Tony Morphet in 1983
that he had "no wish to enter the lists as a defender of Michael K" (Morphet
459). However, he has responded directly to Gordimer's objections:

> What kind of model of behavior in the face of oppression was
> I presenting? Why hadn't I written a different book with (I put
> words in her mouth now) a less spineless hero?
>
> To a reader taking this line, much of the text of *Michael K* is
> just one fancy evasion after another of an overriding political
> question: how shall the tyranny of apartheid be ended?...
>
> How do I respond to such readers?
>
> One writes the books one wants to write. One doesn't write the
> books one doesn't want to write. The emphasis falls not on *one*
> but on the word *want* in all its own resistance to being known.
> The book...in the heroic tradition, is not a book I *wanted-to-write*,
> wanted enough to be able to bring off, however much I might have

wanted to have written it—that is to say, wanted to be the person who had successfully brought off the writing of it.

What, then, do I *want-to-write*? A question to prospect, to open up, perhaps in the present dialogue, but not to mine, to exploit. Too much of the fictional enterprise depends on it. Just as it is not productive to discover the answer to the question of why one desires: the answer threatens the end of desire, the end of the production of desire. (*DP* 207–208)

Coetzee is clear that he has no argument with those who cleave to the heroic tradition. He has always admired Nadine Gordimer—in 1978, he said, "I read Nadine Gordimer because I think she's extraordinarily accomplished" (Watson 22), although he has reservations about her difficulty in accepting "that stories finally have to tell themselves, that the hand that holds the pen is only the conduit of a signifying process" (*DP* 341). He told David Attwell that he regarded it "as a badge of honor to have had a book banned in South Africa, and even more of an honor to have been acted against punitively. … This honor I have never achieved nor, to be frank, merited" (*DP* 298).

Nevertheless, in his most direct contribution to the debate of the 1980s, his 1987 address in Cape Town titled "The Novel Today," he complains that "in South Africa the colonisation of the novel by the discourse of history is proceeding with alarming rapidity" owing to the "intense ideological pressure" of the time (3). He is at pains to point out that storytelling and history are both discourses, neither of which has a monopoly on the representation of reality, and

> no matter what it may appear to be doing, the story may not really be playing the game you call Class Conflict or the game called Male Domination or any of the other games in the games handbook. While it may certainly be possible to read the book as playing one of those games, in reading it in that way you may have missed something. You may have missed not just something, you may have missed everything. (4)

There is a connection between the open-mindedness Coetzee is recommending here to readers and the kind of open-minded, nonanalytical approach he finds necessary for the "fictional enterprise." As a superb literary critic himself, he knows the enterprise from both sides and is wary of confusing the two roles. The deadening hand of reductionism in reading has its twin in the author's attempt to self-censor or to direct stories towards a moral or political goal rather than letting them "tell themselves."

One thing that may be missed by readers looking for political "games" or messages in Coetzee's work is "a certain spirit of resistance" which he hopes is "ingrained in my books" (Morphet 464). This resistance to cooption or interpretation is linked to his feelings about freedom, which I take to be absolutely basic to all his work:

> To be a herald you would have to have slipped your chains for a while and wandered about in the real world. I am not a herald of community or anything else…I am someone who has intimations of freedom (as every chained prisoner has) and constructs representations—which are shadows themselves—of people slipping their chains and turning their faces to the light. I do not imagine freedom, freedom *an sich*; I do not represent it. Freedom is another name for the unimaginable. (*DP* 341)

The chains that his people have slipped are to a large extent representations imposed on them by others. Derek Attridge points out that

> the task Coetzee seems to have set himself is to convey the resistance of these figures to the discourses of the ruling culture…and at the same time to find a means of representing the claims they make upon those who inhabit this culture. (*J. M. Coetzee* 13)

The figures to which Attridge is alluding here are Coetzee's "others"— Michael K, the barbarians, Vercueil in *Age of Iron*. However, resistance of those characters who might be plausibly identified to some extent with the author himself is no small part of Coetzee's vision, especially in his most recent books. A consistent refusal to be enlisted into civil society on its own terms can be found in *Disgrace*, *Elizabeth Costello*, and *Slow Man*, as well as his three fictional memoirs, *Boyhood*, *Youth*, and *Summertime*.

To see how this spirit of resistance might have developed, it may be useful to survey the statements he has made about the place of politics in literature. In 1978, as a relatively little-known author of two novels, he was asked, "Do you believe that South African writers should see themselves as having any definite responsibilities?" He replied,

> I guess so. Let's say that in a way it's easier and more difficult being a writer in South Africa than in West European countries; because there are such gigantic subjects of such unassailable importance facing a writer in South Africa. (Watson 22)

Later in the same interview, however, asked whether "the sense of necessity imposed by the political situation is an inhibiting factor as regards creativity," he replied,

> I myself don't feel that pressure you talk about. It's a matter partly of privilege, partly of temperament; also perhaps a matter of personal history. I spent my twenties outside this country, and really wasn't engaged with the apartheid situation for a long, crucial period of my life. (Watson 23)

In 1985, with a Booker Prize to his name, he is more cautious about answering questions about the responsibilities of writers:

> As to the question of the role of the writer, there seems to be a model behind the question, a model of a social structure in which people are assigned roles to play, and I am not sure that I would agree with the model underlying the question. I would have to be convinced that such roles are assigned, and by whom. (Sévry 1)

These seem to be the words of a writer who has been asked these questions too often and who has become practiced at responding more carefully. Implicit in these words, we might read a reaction to Gordimer's review of *Life & Times of Michael K* quoted earlier. Clearly, he is beginning to resist attempts like Gordimer's to assert her authority and that of her own guiding authorities such as Lukács over his work. Nevertheless, later in the same interview, he was asked about the apparent conflict between aesthetic approaches to literature and politics in South Africa, "as if literature was something the European writer could afford, whereas the non-European couldn't." His response was blunt:

> I know the argument. But there is finally a test that all writing must certainly submit to: who is going to read it. One of these days there will be a major black talent who will do the aesthetic exploration and write revolutionary literature. They are not incompatible and people who say they are incompatible are simply mistaken. (Sévry 7)

In 1987 came the "Novel Today" talk, where he envisaged history and fiction, in a vivid metaphor, as existing side by side "like two cows on the same pasture, each minding its own business," but which were by the present exigencies of South Africa being squeezed together so that fiction was left with "only two options: supplementarity or rivalry." Does this imply a change of attitude? Is revolutionary literature necessarily the type of "supplementary" literature he describes, which "aims to provide the reader with vicarious first-hand experience of living in a certain historical time, embodying contending forces in contending characters and filling our experience with a certain density of observation," and thus incompatible with "aesthetic exploration" after all ("Novel" 3)? In uncharacteristically dramatic language, he described the relationship between history, with its subdiscourse of politics, on the one hand, and storytelling on the other, as "a battlefield" ("Novel" 3).

Only a few years later, in the interviews with David Attwell published in *Doubling the Point* in 1992, Coetzee is more introspective, partly because of the different context—the difference between a public speech and a conversation with a colleague—but also reflecting a change in the situation. He still complains that the "discourse about what people *are* writing in South Africa slides so easily nowadays into discourse about what people *ought to be* writing. It's an arid discourse that I take no joy in, particularly when it sideslips into polemics." But the stirring rhetoric of battlefields is absent, and his diffidence is reinforced by the way he describes himself in the context of the anti-imperialist struggle of his youth:

> The picture of myself marching to the fray—I, with my crav-
> ing for privacy, my distaste for crowds, for slogans, my almost
> physical revulsion against obeying orders, I who by dint of utterly
> uncharacteristic, single-minded cunning had got through four
> years of high school without doing military drill—the picture was
> simply comic. (*DP* 337)

From this remarkable piece of introspection, we might conclude that the debate, though no doubt an irritant, had little effect on him as a writer. His personality—antiauthoritarian and fastidious—was formed long before he gave any thought to a writer's duties and responsibilities.

The debate itself no doubt continues at some level, but in 1997, when Joanna Scott asked him about the "angry divisions" in South Africa "between social realism and modernist or experimental fiction," Coetzee replied that "the particularly strident polemic you mention between social realism and so called experimental or modernist or even postmodernist fiction is largely obsolete now. ... Thankfully, the debate has shifted into a more nuanced and complex mode" (Scott 98). For her part, Gordimer wrote the preface to *Critical Perspectives on J. M. Coetzee* in 1996, and she seems to have revised her judgment on Michael K. While in her 1984 review, she implied that he was not suf-ficiently representative of "the black people of South Africa," she now says, "Michael K was one of them, all of them." She points out that despite that fact that some of Coetzee's fiction does not make explicit mention of South Africa, it "could not have come from anywhere else in the world," and further, that his fiction makes the "demand on intellect, morals and mores" which is the only proof of any fiction's worth, "with rare authority" (Preface xi). It would be too dramatic to say a truce has been declared, but the debate is clearly no longer significant to either Gordimer or Coetzee.

* * * * *

There is some argument about whether *Boyhood* (1997) and *Youth* (2002) are in fact autobiographical. *Boyhood* bears the subtitle *A Memoir* in several editions, while others are labeled *Scenes from Provincial Life*, and the New York publisher's press release describes the book as "a revealing and moving account of his childhood in South Africa" (Slovak). The first U.S. edition of *Youth* is subtitled *Scenes from Provincial Life II* to match *Boyhood*, but the British edition and other subsequent editions have no subtitle, as if Coetzee wants to withdraw his identification with the "John Coetzee" who is the main character in *Youth*: the blurb in the first British edition gives nothing away, guardedly talking about "the narrator of *Youth*, a student in the South Africa of the 1950s."[1] It is notable that *Youth* ends in 1964 with John unmarried, while Coetzee married in 1963 (The Nobel Foundation). *Summertime*, the third in the "Scenes from Provincial Life" series, confuses the picture even further. The famous writer John Coetzee is dead, and a biographer who never met him is gathering information from various sources. There is clearly one major fictional element here, and there are sure to be many others. There is a somewhat similar problem with *Diary of a Bad Year*, which concerns an elderly, world-famous South African writer with the initials J. C. who has recently migrated to Australia. In this case, there are several definite clues to distinguish the character J. C. from J. M. Coetzee: his age, for example—seventy-two in 2005, while Coetzee turned sixty-five that year—and the fact that he lives in Sydney rather than Adelaide. However, as Dominic Head suggests, the memoirs "enrich our understanding of the author's life—or, at least his chosen self-projection."[2] *Boyhood*, *Youth*, and *Summertime* all follow closely the known history of Coetzee's life; date of birth (though not of marriage or death), education, and so on all correspond, and one could be forgiven for assuming that a memoir, even if it is fictionalized, by a novelist of international stature must be intended to some extent as an account of his development as a novelist.

What we see emerging in *Boyhood* is a consciousness that questions everything and, while admitting allegiance where it is absolutely unavoidable, to his mother, for example, it does so grudgingly and with full awareness of the contradictions involved. His love for his mother is a "fierce and angry emotion...It is because he is so sure of her care that he is on his guard with her, never relaxing, never allowing her a chance." But he understands his cruelty: "Feeling her hurt...he knows he is in a trap and cannot get out. *Love*: this is what love really is, this cage in which he rushes back and forth, back and forth, like a poor bewildered baboon" (*B* 122). He does take sides when absolutely necessary. He chooses the unpopular Russians over the Americans in the Cold War: "He chose the Russians in 1947 when everyone else was choosing the Americans," realizing only later that "liking Russians was not part of a game, it was not allowed." So he learns: from a childish, contrary urge at the age of seven to support the less popular side, he discovers that "whatever he wants, whatever he likes, has sooner or later to be turned into a secret" (*B* 27–28). It is significant, though, that this does not make him change his mind about what he likes, even though the original choice might have been made without much thought. He merely becomes like a trapdoor spider, "always...scuttling back into its hole, closing the trapdoor behind it, shutting out the world, hiding" (*B* 28). He doesn't want to change: "In that case he would no longer be himself. If he were no longer himself, what point would there be in living?" (*B* 35).

His identity is constantly in question. "He thinks of himself as English. Though his surname is Afrikaans, though his father is more Afrikaans than English, though he himself speaks Afrikaans without any English accent, he could not pass for a moment as an Afrikaner" (*B* 124). But, faced with "proper English boys, with English names," despite "the English language which he commands with ease" and "England and everything that England stands for, to which he believes he is loyal," he realizes that "more than that is required, clearly, before one will be accepted as truly English: tests to face, some of which he knows he will not pass" (*B* 129). His constant fear is that he will be relegated to Afrikaans classes at school because of his surname and will be forced to share the classroom with the Afrikaners he shrinks away from, with their "surliness...intransigence, and, not far behind it...threat of physical force" (*B* 124). So his sense of racial identity, in a society where race is an integral part of everyone's self-image, is confused: all he knows is that he doesn't unequivocally belong with any group.

In religion, his family is "certainly nothing" (*B* 18), which causes bleakly comic difficulties at school, where one must belong to one of the three categories: Christian, Roman Catholic, or Jew. Belonging is something Coetzee only gives himself to wholeheartedly in respect to his uncle's farm. He feels that he belongs on and even to the farm, though it will never belong to him and he knows "he will never be more than a guest, an uneasy guest" (*B* 79). He is conscious that his father's family, whom he despises for their "life of dull, stupid formulas, of being like everyone else" (*B* 79), for reasons not entirely clear but the subject of brooding speculation, resents him and his mother and that he is not completely welcome on his beloved farm, the farm which he knows will be lost to him forever one day.

All this adds up to a sensibility with few certainties, a wary, prickly, preternaturally observant boy who has to hold himself constantly in check and who questions the basis of everything. Although he has a romantic vision of himself as "different, special...waiting to be called" (*B* 108), the cause in which he is to be enlisted is obscure. Perhaps some hint of it is contained in the final pages of the book. His great-aunt Annie dies, leaving behind her a storeroom full of copies of her father's book, which she had spent her life translating, publishing, and trying to sell. John finds the book too boring to read and knows that his great-grandfather, the author, was "a terrible old German, terribly cruel and autocratic" (*B* 118). Nevertheless, after Aunt Annie's death, he wonders about the books, which everyone else has forgotten. "He alone is left to do the thinking. How will he keep them all in his head, all the books, all the people, all the stories? And if he does not remember them, who will?" (*B* 166). This is the end of *Boyhood*, and it sounds like the declaration of a vocation. It sounds like a reluctant acknowledgment of a dedication to a cause which even he finds boring or unpleasant, but to which he has committed himself. In the same vein, in his 1984 essay "Remembering Texas," he recalls his studies in so-called primitive languages. Finding that "every one of the 700 tongues of Borneo was as coherent and complex and intractable to analysis as English," he wondered

> if a latter-day ark were ever commissioned to take the best that mankind has to offer and make a fresh start on the farther planets... might we not leave Shakespeare's plays and Beethoven's quartets behind to make room for the last speaker of Dyirbal, even though that last speaker might be a fat old woman who scratched herself and smelled bad? (*DP* 52–53)

It is only a question, but implicit in the question is the resistance to cultural and social imperatives which surfaces periodically throughout his work. Of course, Coetzee is not a philistine. His resistance to received opinion is not a rejection of the objects of that opinion—of Shakespeare and Beethoven, although we see from *Youth* that, at least when young, he preferred the solitary savagery of Swift (*Y* 21), and the intricate, intellectual music of J. S. Bach holds greater appeal for him (*SS* 8; *DBY* 173). Individual tastes aside, this is a larger attitude that steps back and allows room to consider points of view which not only do not occur to most other people, but would be regarded by many with horrified dismay.

In *Youth*, the ten-year-old who had shouted "I hate normal people" (*B* 78) at his mother has become a teenager so alienated from other people that he can form normal relations with no one. At nineteen, he is living alone in Cape Town, a student precariously but stubbornly independent of his family. His only ambition is to be a poet, and his every thought is directed towards discovering the poet's mode of being. Over the five years covered in *Youth*, in Cape Town and then in England, he gropes his way through life guided only by literature. T. S. Eliot and Ezra Pound are his principal mentors, and Ford Madox Ford, admired by Pound, on whom he is writing a dutiful but increasingly disenchanted master's thesis. Unable to establish any friendships, behaving shamefully to the women he sleeps with, he is immersed in misery: "[I]f misery were to be abolished, he would not know what to do with himself" (*Y* 65). Luckily, there seems to be no question of that: he is occasionally ambushed by joy—the word is used twice in *Youth*—but misery returns to claim him soon enough. The few flashes of delight are sparked mainly by literature. Firstly, he discovers Joseph Brodsky, Ingeborg Bachmann, and Zbigniew Herbert, who tell him "of what poetry can be and therefore of what he can be, filling him with joy that he inhabits the same earth as they" (*Y* 91). Later, when he has begun to think that prose might suit his talents better than poetry, he reads Samuel Beckett's *Watt*, which is "so funny that he rolls about laughing" (*Y* 155). Laughing! Nothing in the previous 150 pages has prepared us for laughter. At last, he has found a model: "How could he have imagined he wanted to write in the manner of Ford when Beckett was around all the time?...Beckett is classless, or outside class, as he himself would prefer to be" (*Y* 155).

Earlier, he had found books in the British Museum, accounts of "the South Africa of the old days" (*Y* 137), which give him the idea of writing a book about South Africa, "a book whose horizon of knowledge will be that of...the 1820s" (*Y* 138). Years later, this idea grew into the second part of his first novel, *Dusklands*. But the "ugly new South Africa" (*Y* 137) still repels him. He has left Cape Town for London hurriedly to escape being drafted into military service after the Sharpeville massacre and is under no illusions about the welcome to be expected in England by "forlorn South African whites cluttering their doorstep like orphans in search of parents" (*Y* 87). His solution to the problem of South Africa is a Russian invasion: "They should land paratroops in Pretoria, take Verwoerd and his cronies captive, line them up against a wall, and shoot them." He is not concerned about what happens then: "Justice must be done, that is all that matters; the rest is politics, and he is not interested in politics" (*Y* 100). He attends a Campaign for Nuclear Disarmament rally, but "fist-shaking and slogan-chanting, the whipping up of passion in general, repel him. Only love and art are, in his opinion, worthy of giving oneself to without reserve" (*Y* 85). Love and art must be taken seriously: he disapproves of flirting, and throughout a course of dancing lessons, "he remained rigid with resistance" (*Y* 89). He seems above all afraid of losing control. The watchfulness he learned as a child can rarely be relaxed, though one Sunday afternoon in spring on Hampstead Heath, he "sinks into a sleep or half-sleep in which consciousness does not vanish but continues to hover. ... At last it has come, the moment of ecstatic unity with the All!" The ironic tone, though still lingering, abates for a moment: "If he has not utterly been transfigured, then at least he has been blessed with a hint that he belongs on this earth" (*Y* 117). From here, we might expect some improvement, and indeed, John finds a computer pro-gramming job which he finds absorbing after the drab misery of his work at IBM. But disenchantment returns: he cannot get started with the writing which he believes will define his life, and Love is as distant a prospect as ever. The book ends on a passively suicidal note, "locked into an attenuating endgame, playing himself, with each move, further into a corner and into defeat" (*Y* 169).

In *Boyhood* and even more in *Youth*, the narrative is peppered with question marks. The young John's uncertainty about what to feel makes him a continual questioner, and despite the relentless misery, the ques-tions create a comic effect, the irony directed by the writer against his beleaguered younger self. Both books are written in the third person, increasing the ironic detachment the older Coetzee assumes: as Head points out, "Coetzee contrives to depict his youthful self in as poor a light as possible" (*Cambridge* 15). Even the hopelessness of the end-ing of *Youth* is comic, especially since the reader knows of the literary triumphs ahead. Choosing to end there, rather than earlier with one of John's moments of surprised happiness, or later with the beginnings of success, is certainly an artistic decision. A note of hopefulness at the end would not suit the book's overall tone and would, strangely, under-mine the humor, which is based upon the young John's self-conscious resistance to anything which might interfere with his poetic vocation or betray his dour self-image as heir to

> the stubborn, mean lives that his ancestors lived, sweating in the heat and dust of the Karoo. ... It was not in the nature of those men and women to be gay and have pleasure, and it is not in his. He is their child, foredoomed from birth to be gloomy and suffer. How else does poetry come anyway, except out of suffering, like blood squeezed from a stone? (*Y* 116)

Youth has an epigraph which might be read in several ways. It comes from Goethe:

> *Wer den Dichter will verstehen*
> *muß in Dichters Lande gehen.*
> [Whoever wants to understand the poet must go to the poet's
>   country.]

Is the *Dichter* (poet) who is to be understood Coetzee himself? Are we, in *Youth*, to be taken into Coetzee's *Lande* in order to understand him, his *Lande* being the territory of his mind? Or is it a statement of what the young John was trying to do—enter the country of his favorite poets, Eliot and Pound, in order to understand them? Whichever way we take it, it is of course essential to remember that this memoir and its predecessor, *Boyhood*, were written years later, and however accurate or otherwise their accounts of the time might be, they are shaped to a purpose. Self-revelation has never been a favorite activity with him, and exactly why Coetzee wrote them will probably always be something of a mystery on which one might waste endless speculation. But whatever their purpose or motivation, they show the development of that stubborn spirit of resistance which has nothing to do with politics but sometimes seems almost to amount to a rejection of life in all its variety, with the trust in others and oneself and the compromises which it constantly demands. A rueful recognition of this tendency can be found in *Diary of a Bad Year*:

> As a young man, I never for a moment allowed myself to doubt that only from a self disengaged from the mass and critical of the mass could true art emerge. Whatever art has come from my hand has in one way or another expressed and even gloried in this disengagement. But what sort of art has that been, in the end? Art that is not great-souled, as the Russians would say, that lacks generosity, fails to celebrate life, lacks love. (*DBY* 138)

Despite the fact that this is a novel rather than a personal diary, one can surely hear the voice of the author here. He goes too far, however.

His writing does not lack love or fail to celebrate life, but does so with a clear-eyed skepticism that is far more bracing and valuable than the optimism of many more deliberately celebratory works. Despite their desperation, there is a vitality in survivors like Michael K and the Magistrate, and *Diary of a Bad Year* goes a long way towards a more generous spirit of harmony and reconciliation, with an unexpected mutual trustfulness and regard growing up between J. C. as he approaches death and the young and vital Anya.

Nevertheless, resistance, in the sense of rejecting, or at least questioning, the claims of society that are unthinkingly followed by most people, is ingrained in Coetzee's fiction. In the earlier books, it was assumed by most critics that this was a reaction to the political situation in South Africa:

> Almost from the beginning, his novels struck one as ways of escape from the most immediate contexts, the South African, in which they were produced. ... The more oppressive conditions of life in South Africa were to become—and these conditions have hardly relented, even at the time of writing [1996]—the more transcendent, one might say, became the formal impulses of his novels, the more profound the misery and revolt of their protagonists. No matter what, it would seem that Coetzee could not help building into his novels certain spaces (or, perhaps, places of refuge) which might or might not exist, but which were designed to elude the dead-weight of South African life in the 1970s and 1980s. (Huggan and Watson 3)

Most clearly seen in *From the Heart of the Country*, *Waiting for the Barbarians*, *Age of Iron*, and *Life & Times of Michael K*, this spirit of rejection, the impulse to slip the chains of what is expected even though the consequences are an even greater bondage, might be viewed, however obliquely, as a political stance. But what of David Lurie's resistance in *Disgrace*? His refusal to defend himself or to even try to soften the consequences of his sexual misdeeds can hardly be regarded as a noble political crusade, although there is a certain obstinate nobility in the penance he submits himself to. From the beginning, he realizes that "he must grit his teeth and pay, what else?" for his brief liaison with his student Melanie. But he refuses to cooperate with the compromise suggested by the university's disciplinary board, the "prudent" approach which might save his job—undergoing counseling, making statements to "demonstrate his sincerity," all the mealy-mouthed pieties of modern sociopsychology. He complains to his daughter, "It reminds me too much of Mao's China. Recantation, self-criticism, public apology. I'm old-fashioned, I would prefer simply to be put against a wall and shot" (*D* 66). So he loses his job, a matter of little regret in the rationalized university of the 1990s, where his interest in the Romantic poets was barely tolerated in the new discipline of communications that has replaced classics and modern languages. He visits his daughter on her small farm, far from Cape Town, and at the end of the novel is working in an animal refuge, helping to put unwanted dogs down and dispose of their remains in the way he regards as fitting:

> Why has he taken on this job?…
> For his idea of the world, a world in which men do not use shovels to beat corpses into a more convenient shape for processing. …
> Curious that a man as selfish as he should be offering himself to the service of dead dogs. There must be other, more productive ways of giving oneself to the world, or to an idea of the world. …
> He saves the honour of corpses because there is no one else stupid enough to do it. That is what he is becoming: stupid, daft, wrongheaded. (*D* 145–146)

Is it a penance, one which he can accept because it is self-imposed? Or does he identify with the dogs, disposed of because they have no place in the modern human world, with their natural but inconvenient desires? He tries to explain to Lucy:

> One can punish a dog, it seems to me, for an offence like chewing a slipper. A dog will accept the justice of that: a beating for a chewing. But desire is another story. No animal will accept the justice of being punished for following its instincts. (*D* 90)

Comedy

Nevertheless, he submits himself to "a state of disgrace from which it will not be easy to lift myself. ... I am living it out from day to day, trying to accept disgrace as my state of being" (*D* 172).

So far, *Disgrace* has little to say directly about the politics of the new South Africa, where the novel is set. However, his daughter Lucy's stubborn resistance to reporting her rape by three black intruders or to taking any steps to guard against its recurrence certainly has a political aspect. She wants to stay on her farm, even though she expects that the rapists will return. "What if...*that* is the price one has to pay for staying on? Perhaps that is how they look at it; perhaps that is how I should look at it too" (*D* 158). Her refusal to be prudent in someone else's terms, of course, parallels his, but as a father, he cannot happily witness her obstinate vulnerability. "If she had any sense she would quit," he says, echoing her own advice to him: "You shouldn't be so unbending, David. It isn't heroic to be unbending" (*D* 66). She finally accepts an offer from her neighbor and former helper Petrus to become his third wife in return for his protection: "I agree, it is humiliating," she tells her father.

> "But perhaps that is a good point to start from again. Perhaps that is what I must learn to accept. To start at ground level. With nothing. Not with nothing but. With nothing. No cards, no weapons, no property, no rights, no dignity."
> "Like a dog," he responds. (*D* 205)

There is little comedy in *Disgrace*, though David Lurie has a strong defensive sense of his own ridiculousness, and the chamber opera he is writing, *Byron in Italy*, surprises him by becoming a comedy: "It is not the erotic that is calling to him after all, nor the elegiac, but the comic," surely mirroring to some extent the ludicrousness of his own postdisgrace life (*D* 184). Coetzee's next novel, *Elizabeth Costello*, begins somberly, if not grimly, with the aging, tired novelist making unsuitable speeches in various settings. Her passions are all out of step with her audiences: animal rights, vegetarianism, the problem of evil in literature—her views are not received with enthusiasm despite her reputation (based, gallingly, mainly on a novel she wrote in the 1960s). But, like a true Coetzee heroine, she resists giving her audience what they want, even pulling the rug from under their polite acquiescence. Having silenced the room by announcing at an academic dinner that her vegetarianism arises "out of a desire to save my soul," she then further alienates the one person who expresses respect for her "way of life" by responding, "I'm wearing leather shoes…I'm carrying a leather purse. I wouldn't have overmuch respect if I were you" (*EC* 89). She is in turn rejected, or stonewalled, by Paul West, the novelist whose book *The Very Rich Hours of Count von Stauffenberg* (1980) she is about to attack in her paper "Witness, Silence, and Censorship" at an international conference in Amsterdam. She tries to explain herself to him in private beforehand, but although he hears her out, he makes no sign, speaks no word, in response. After her paper, she sees two alternatives—to stay at the conference or leave, but

> there ought to be a third alternative, some way of rounding off the morning and giving it shape and meaning: some confrontation leading to some final word. There ought to be an arrangement such that she bumps into someone in the corridor, perhaps Paul West himself; something should pass between them, sudden as lightning, that will illuminate the landscape for her, even if afterwards it returns to its native darkness. But the corridor, it seems, is empty. (*EC* 182)

No neat conclusions for Coetzee's characters: their resistance, heroic or otherwise, is not to be rewarded with illuminations and resolutions.

But the last of the eight "lessons" in this "novel," if not exactly light-hearted, at least tends towards the lighter end of the spectrum. Elizabeth Costello is confronted with what will presumably be her final challenge, "At the Gate." To pass through the gate, she must make a statement of beliefs, but she is not prepared to do so: "I am a writer, a trader in fictions…I maintain beliefs only provisionally: fixed beliefs would stand in my way" (*EC* 195). This, however, is unacceptable to the authorities, and she is stranded in a world where a parody of Kafka jostles grotesquely with a comic-opera pastiche, trying to reconcile her skepticism with the requirement that she believe in something. Eventually, she remembers—or creates—a story about frogs in her Australian childhood which she can believe:

> Today, at this time, in this place, she is evidently not without belief. In fact, now that she thinks of it, she lives, in a certain sense, by belief. Her mind, when she is truly herself, appears to pass from one belief to the next, pausing, balancing, then moving on…She lives by belief, she is a creature of belief. What a relief! (*EC* 222)

The relief seems more than merely temporary satisfaction at being able to make a sincere statement to the demanding judges so she can pass through her gate. But there are many layers of irony here, and they can be peeled back as far as the reader wishes. Perhaps the resistance that is so much a part of Coetzee's repertoire is ultimately skepticism: if you don't accept the usual beliefs of your society, whether they concern sexual morality, censorship, or the rights of animals, you are bound to resist the rules and sanctions which arise from those beliefs. For David and Lucy Lurie, this means a difficult life of hardship and risk; for Elizabeth Costello, after the trials of old age, it means endless days "in a kind of literary theme park." At the end of the novel, she is still waiting to be allowed through to something which she is not convinced is worth the wait: "There is light, certainly, but it is not the light that Dante saw in Paradise, it is not even in the same league" (*EC* 209).

And in *Slow Man*, what are we to make of Paul Rayment's graceless refusal to be helped? When Michael K says, "I have escaped the camps; perhaps, if I lie low, I will escape the charity too" (*MK* 18), it could conceivably be a reaction to political circumstances, but when Rayment refuses a prosthesis to replace his amputated leg, it seems to arise from nothing but a temperamental reaction to bad luck. He knows he is behaving badly: "A golden opportunity was presented to him to set an example of how one accepts with good cheer one of the bitterer blows of fate, and he has spurned it" (*SM* 15). It is partly a matter of style: he is old-fashioned, like David Lurie, and rejects the very idea of a prosthesis: "He shudders at the thought of it; he wants nothing to do with it. Crutches are better. Crutches are at least honest. … 'I don't want to look natural,' he says. 'I prefer to feel natural'" (*SM* 58–59). His nurse Marijana is the only person who can lift him off his high horse: "He would like her to think he bears his mishap gamely; he would like her to think well of him in all respects" (*SM* 30).

The novel seems to be developing as a reasonably straightforward realist story about an uncooperative injured man with unsuitable feelings towards his nurse. Then Elizabeth Costello arrives on his doorstep, and the fiction starts to turn on itself. Rayment's resistance to the ramifications of his condition remains, but his energies are now focused on rebelling against this novelist, who knows all about him and the other people in his life and keeps urging him to act in some dramatic way. He suspects that she "is at work on a new book, and seems to be using me in it as a character, so to speak" (*SM* 141).

Costello's urging is an irritant but does not seriously affect Rayment's behavior, and despite her eloquence, he is "signally unmoved":

> "Mrs Costello," he says, "please open your ears to what I am saying. What is going on between myself and Drago's family [Drago is Marijana's teenage son] is none of your business. You do not belong here. This is not your place, not your sphere. I feel for Marijana. I feel for Drago, in a different way, and for his sisters too. I can even feel for Drago's father. But I cannot feel for you. None of us is able to feel for you. You are the one outsider among us. Your involvement, however well-meaning it may be, does not help us, merely confuses us." (*SM* 263)

The implications of this for the relationship between a writer and his characters are both comic and tinged with pathos, at least from the writer's point of view. When Rayment finally manages to reject her, to send her away, at the end of the novel, Costello asks, "'But what am I going to do without you?' She seems to be smiling, but her lips are trembling too" (*SM* 263). After a long line of characters resisting the demands of society, Coetzee has now turned his attention to what would happen within a fiction if a character were to resist his creator. A dramatization of writer's

block, or a philosophical meditation on a writer's rights and responsibilities? Both, probably, but the most striking thing about *Slow Man* is
its playfulness. Paul Rayment finds some of Elizabeth Costello's novels in the local public library, and his reaction is, predictably, irritable.
He discovers that her most famous book is about Marion Bloom from
James Joyce's *Ulysses*: "What is wrong with her? Can she not make up
characters on her own?" The humor becomes almost broad: "*Why, why?
Why does she ask a question and then not give the answer?*" (*SM* 119).
Questions without answers make up much of Rayment's narrative, and
indeed, like the use of characters he has not made up on his own, they
have featured frequently in Coetzee's fiction. Once again, as in *Elizabeth
Costello*, the ironies come in multiple layers.

The use of rhetorical questions often has a comic effect. It can also
be a way of expressing skepticism. In a world where nothing is given,
every belief or position may be questioned, and when everything may be
questioned, of course, there are no reliable guides to behavior. This conclusion might be interpreted as an invitation to complete freedom from
restraint and morality. However, in Coetzee's world, freedom becomes
the right to resist any external set of values while rigorously following
an internal compass, based apparently on instinct, even while its assumptions are also subjected to the same kind of skeptical questioning as any
other value system. Coetzee's freedom becomes the freedom to question
and to resist without a duty to justify one's resistance. In *Diary of a Bad
Year*, the aging South African writer J. C. is one of several who have
been invited by a German publisher to deliver themselves of opinions
"on any subjects they choose, the more contentious the better" (*DBY* 20).
J. C. writes with brooding skepticism about anarchism and the origins
of the state, about the war on terror and Australian politics, but also on
probability and Zeno's paradox and intelligent design.

> If I were pressed to give my brand of political thought a label, I
> would call it pessimistic anarchistic quietism, or anarchist qui-
> etistic pessimism, or pessimistic quietistic anarchism: anarchism
> because experience tells me that what is wrong with politics is

> power itself; quietism because I have my doubts about the will
> to set about changing the world, a will infected with the drive to
> power; and pessimism because I am sceptical that, in a fundamen-
> tal way, things can be changed. ...
>
> But do I really qualify as a thinker at all, someone who has
> what can properly be called thoughts, about politics or about any-
> thing else? I have never been easy with abstractions or good at
> abstract thoughts. (*DBY* 160)

A writer who has clearly and methodically dismantled the philosophical
basis for statehood and democracy is being too modest here. However,
his reservations about expressing such opinions have grown as the book
develops: "I survey my elderly coevals and see all too many consumed
with grouchiness, all too many who allow their helpless bafflement about
the way things are going to turn into the main theme of their final years"
(*DBY* 121), and his opinions are balanced by the political apathy and
personal warmth of the youthful Anya. But, he notes, "what has begun
to change since I moved into the orbit of Anya is not my opinions themselves so much as my opinion of my opinions" (106–107). He has not
changed his mind about the world. Rather, he can see another point of
view from which his own would seem "alien and antiquated" (107–108).
He has come to be skeptical about his skepticism.

Early in *Summertime*, Coetzee seems to be following the same path of
self-questioning, almost in a parody of *Youth* and *Diary of a Bad Year*.
Faced with the apparent indifference of his father to the crimes of the
South African Nationalist government in 1972, he wonders, in the notebook entry which begins the book, whether "his own response—fits of
rage and despair—[is] any better?" (*S* 5). However, this is mild com-
pared to what follows. As the biographer, Mr. Vincent, interviews his
chosen witnesses to John Coetzee's time in South Africa in the early
1970s, he finds them prepared, even eager, to demolish any notion of
him as a progressive thinker or, indeed, as remarkable in any way. The
self-image (many times refracted) presented here is earnest and ineffectual. As in *Elizabeth Costello*, vegetarianism is the occasion of social
awkwardness. The question comes up at a family dinner, and, quizzed

by his sharp-tongued cousin Carol, all John can say is, "Not a strict vegetarian. … It is not a word he is fond of. If one chooses not to eat so much meat…" (*S* 94). Tongue-tied by her malicious curiosity, he has to be saved by Margie's mild, "[W]e all have our preferences" (*S* 94). In this case, the discomfort is his, while Elizabeth Costello manages to cast it back on the other diners. The character John makes principled decisions which often turn out to be absurd. Stranded with his cousin Margie on a deserted road in his broken-down truck, the excuse he offers is that

> I try to do things myself when I ought really to leave them to more competent hands. It's because of the country we live in…Because of the long history of making other people do our work for us while we sit in the shade and watch. (*S* 111)

However, although his skills at motor maintenance are lacking, he recounts in his notebook a certain satisfaction in the laborious concreting job he has undertaken to save his house from disintegration: "What he finds himself doing is what people like him should have been doing ever since 1652, namely, his own dirty work." And further, "The slabs he is laying will outlast his tenancy of the house, may even outlast his spell on earth; in which case he will in a certain sense have cheated death" (*S* 7). Why, he thinks, does he bother to keep writing if immortality can be achieved so readily? Then a deflating italicized comment (later glossed by the biographer as Coetzee's own notes from 1999 or 2000) follows: "*To be expanded on: his readiness to throw himself into half-baked projects; the alacrity with which he retreats from creative work into mindless industry*" (*S* 8). As an exercise in self-presentation, *Summertime*, as might be expected, manages to complicate any impression of a man who bases his actions on strong principles. There are rumors that he left the United States after trouble with the law in connection with Vietnam War protests, but that is never clarified. The course in African literature he runs with Sophie Denoël at the University of Cape Town "did not attract the more radical black students. Our approach would have been too academic for them, not *engagé* enough" (*S* 223). John, in *Summertime*, certainly has strong political views, but he has no impulse to activism except on a rather pointless individual level, where it might equally be viewed as stubborn resistance to social convention. And it is surely significant that, despite the political concerns noted in his diary entries at the beginning and end of the book, this "memoir" set in apartheid-era South Africa is otherwise concerned almost exclusively with John's personal life—his sexual and family relationships—rather than the larger social issues one might expect from a liberal-minded writer of good conscience.

Coetzee could not avoid being formed by the circumstances of his childhood and youth. It is nonsensical to ask what kind of writer he would have become had he been born in Australia or Sweden in 1940 rather than in South Africa. But many people were born in South Africa in 1940, and there is still only one J. M. Coetzee. One unwary interviewer asked him whether the "differences in tone, subject matter and approach between your work and another well-known political novelist, Milan Kundera…could…be due to the qualitative differences in the sort of political oppression you write about." Coetzee replied, "I would hope that the differences between Kundera and myself that you mention are due to the fact that we are two different people, not to the grindings and groanings of history in Prague or Pretoria" (Chon 6). As he said later in the same interview, "I have no interest in overtly political literature." (Chon 6). Politics is for those who have firmer ground to stand on; resistance, on the other hand, can originate from the most isolated individual consciousness possessing nothing but the freedom to think for itself.

ENDNOTES

1. Cover notes to Coetzee, *Youth*.
2. Head, *Cambridge* 1. Head is referring to *Boyhood* and *Youth* here, as *Summertime* is not included in his study.

CHAPTER 3

POINT OF VIEW

COMPLICITY, REALISM, ISOLATION

Coetzee's Elizabeth Costello, making her statement to "the ultimate tribunal" to which she is required to state her beliefs, tells the judges that she is, in Czeslaw Milosz's phrase, "a secretary of the invisible."

> "Every morning I seat myself at my desk and ready myself for the summons of the day. That is a secretary's way of life, and mine. ...
>
> "A word of caution to you, however. I am open to all voices, not just the voices of the murdered and violated. ... If it is their murderers and violators who choose to summon me instead, to use me and speak through me, I will not close my ears to them, I will not judge them. ...
>
> "Do you think the guilty do not suffer too?" she says. "Do you think they do not call out from their flames? *Do not forget me!*— that is what they cry. What kind of conscience is it that will disregard a cry of such moral agony?" (*EC* 203–204)

The relationship between Coetzee and his character Costello in *Elizabeth Costello* and elsewhere will be more fully canvassed later in this chapter. Meanwhile, suffice to say that naturally, one must not conflate Coetzee and Costello. Furthermore, Costello sees the argument she is proposing here as forming part of the closing stages of "a contest of rhetoric," bringing its status as an authoritative statement even by the character into question (204). However, there is a germ of continuity here with Coetzee's own novelistic practice, especially in his first novel, *Dusklands*. Ok ....

The relationship between author and character in first-person narratives is a complex one. It has become a critical commonplace to assume that first-person narrators are unreliable. The question, then, becomes a matter of degree. If we cannot assume that first-person narrators speak simply on behalf of their authors, it does not follow that their testimony is in every case to be completely rejected. One of the pleasures and challenges of reading first-person narratives lies in discovering the *degree* of reliability of each narrator.

Coetzee's first three novels have first-person narrators, and all are positioned quite differently in relation to their author. In part 1 of *Dusklands*, "The Vietnam Project," the distance between the narrator and main character, Eugene Dawn, and Coetzee as author is manifest immediately. It is surely in a rather playful spirit that Coetzee gives Eugene's antagonist, a "powerful, genial, ordinary man, so utterly without vision" (*DL* 1), his own surname, so that the reader is presented in the second line of the book with a dislocation in identification which serves unequivocally to establish this distance. This is complicated by Eugene's consciousness of himself as an artist pitted against the character Coetzee, whom he regards as "a failed creative person who lives vicariously off true creative people" (*DL* 1). It would be a mistake to see the character Coetzee, as sensible as he appears to be when refracted through the warped lens of Eugene's mind, as simply embodying the author Coetzee's point of view. It would be equally wrong to discount in Eugene's febrile imaginings any correspondence at all with his author's sensibilities. They are, after all, both artists.

Nevertheless, Eugene's sensibility is a ludicrous caricature of the artistic temperament, in which all the normal inhibitions and constraints are removed and the self rules all: "I need coddling. I am an egg that must lie in the downiest of nests under the most coaxing of nurses before my bald, unpromising shell cracks and my shy secret life emerges. Allowances must be made for me" (*DL* 1). The truly savage irony of this narrative emerges when we discover that Eugene's "creative" project is a report on methods of psychological warfare to be used in the Vietnam War.

Eugene's first-person narration is full of special pleading of the type quoted above. It has moments of transparent megalomania and delusion: "I know my wife well, having contributed much to her making" (*DL* 12). Even the therapy he undergoes after his breakdown is grist for his egomania: "I think they must find me an exceptional patient," he says (*DL* 49). But there are also moments of pathos, such as the final sentence: "I have high hopes of finding whose fault I am" (*DL* 49), which takes leave of the reader in such a way that it is impossible finally to condemn or laugh him away.

Eugene's narrative takes the form of a present-tense monologue rather than a diary, with its explicit fiction of a specific moment of writing. He is engaged in explaining himself to an unnamed reader—perhaps even to himself. Within this narrative is included his official report for the Vietnam Project degenerating towards the end into an appeal addressed to Coetzee: "You must listen. I speak with the voice of things to come" (*DL* 29). His appeal seems to have been ignored or rejected, and in part 4, the pace of the monologue becomes immediate and urgent when, having taken his young son Martin and absconded to a motel room somewhere in California, he is besieged by police and, in a passage of extraordinary and rather horrible power, stabs his son:

> Someone else is screaming. That is my wife Marilyn. … She need not worry, I am all right. … Amazing. I have been hit a terrible blow. How could that happen?…Now I am beginning to be hurt. Now someone is really beginning to hurt me. Amazing. (*DL* 43)

The intimacy of our relationship with Eugene, heightened by the first-person present-tense narrative, gives an insight into the mind of an

PAROBY

intelligent, sensitive, dangerous egomaniac. Eugene's insanity is closely allied with the insanity of the Vietnam War. He himself makes that link: "Since February of 1965 their war has been living its life at my expense" (*DL* 38), and though his assessment is pathological rather than objective, it is not open to us to reject this nexus.

"I would be the last person in the world," said Coetzee, "to claim that writing rids one of complicity" (P. Wood 189). In the second part of *Dusklands*, Coetzee writes in the person of his ancestor. "The Narrative of Jacobus Coetzee" states on its title page that it is "Edited, with an Afterword, by S. J. Coetzee; Translated by J. M. Coetzee." A "Translator's Preface" follows the title page, "explaining" in standard academic style the editorial procedures used and acknowledging the help of colleagues and assistants. Jacobus Coetzee was, in fact, a distant forebear of J. M. Coetzee, while his father was Zacharias Coetzee, not S. J. Coetzee.

Parody is clearly the genre of this piece. However, by placing himself within its fictional boundaries, J. M. Coetzee allows himself to be identified with its content in a very straightforward way. In *Doubling the Point*, when David Attwell asked him about his identification with Afrikaners, while not being confident to say either yes or no to the question "Am I...an Afrikaner?" Coetzee said,

> The whites of South Africa participated, in various degrees, actively or passively, in an audacious and well-planned crime against Africa. Afrikaners as a self-defining group distinguished themselves in the commission of that crime. Thereby they lent their name to it. It will be a long time before they have the moral authority to withdraw that brandmark. ... Is it in my power to withdraw from the gang? I think not. ... More important, is it my heart's desire to withdraw from the gang? Not really. Furthermore—and this is an afterthought—I would regard it as morally questionable to write something like the second part of *Dusklands*—a *fiction*, note—from a position that is not historically complicit. (*DP* 342–343)

"The Narrative of Jacobus Coetzee," then, uses the author's name in a different way from "The Vietnam Project." While "Coetzee" in the first part of the book is on the side of sanity (if also fully implicated in waging the war in Vietnam), the three Coetzees of the second part are engaged in promoting one of the "heroes" of that "audacious and well-planned crime against Africa." Coetzee the author thus puts himself and his forbears firmly in the frame for the excessive and murderous behavior described in "Narrative."

Once the narrative itself begins, Jacobus is revealed almost immediately as a racist with fixed theories about Hottentots ("The Hottentot is locked into the present. He does not care where he comes from or where he is going" [*DL* 58]) and Bushmen ("Heartless as baboons they are, and the only way to treat them is like beasts" [*DL* 58]). The illusion of eighteenth-century prose is not maintained, so despite the careful positioning provided by the "Translator's Preface," the fiction is soon revealed for what it is: a twentieth-century imagining of a subjective account of the actions of a violent, bigoted, but sensitive, imperialist from two hundred years before. Jacobus is prey to an existential angst:

> I am all that I see. Such loneliness!…What is there that is not me? I am a transparent sac with a black core full of images and a gun.
>   The gun stands for the hope that there exists that which is other than oneself
>   . …The gun saves us from the fear that all life is within us. It does so by laying at our feet all the evidence we need of a dying and therefore a living world. (*DL* 79)

The danger of these meditations becomes clear when Jacobus wipes out a Namaqua village and executes his four Hottentot servants in retribution for the crime of being independent and rejecting him from their world, a world which he admits he cannot understand or appreciate.

> Through their deaths I, who after they had expelled me had wandered the desert like a pallid symbol, again asserted my reality. … I have taken it upon myself to be the one to pull the trigger, performing this sacrifice for myself and my countrymen, who exist, and committing upon the dark folk the murders we have all wished. All are guilty, without exception. … Who knows for what unimaginable

> crimes of the spirit they died, through me? God's judgment is just, irreprehensible, and incomprehensible. His mercy pays no heed to merit. I am a tool in the hands of history. (*DL* 106)

But what a strange and enigmatic ending follows:

> I can be seen as superfluous. At present I do not care to inhabit such a point of view; but when the day comes you will find that whether I am alive or dead, whether I ever lived or never was born, has never been of real concern to me. I have other things to think about. (*DL* 107)

How many layers of complexity are packed into this passage? Jacobus Coetzee is in the context of this book a fictional character. But he did exist as a remote ancestor of J. M. Coetzee and a pioneer among the Hottentots in southern Africa. Are we to draw from this ending a warning about carrying literal identification too far or taking it too seriously? Is this, finally, saying that despite all the baggage of historical fact which has been erected around Jacobus, he is to be seen as a fictional character who "never was born?" Certainly, this is supported by the following passage from a 1978 interview:

> Q.   Some have found it incongruous, or implausible should I say, that a frontiersman of the 18th century like Jacobus Coetzee should be delivering such complex, essentially modern meditations on exploration, the myth of the gun etcetera, and perhaps more so that a colonial spinster like Magda [in *From the Heart of the Country*] should speak in a form and tone that is so obviously a product of a modern urban consciousness. How would you reply to such a criticism?
> A.   I would reply to a criticism like that by saying that (a) Jacobus Coetzee is not an 18th century frontiersman and (b) Magda is not a colonial spinster.
> Q.   Who are they then?
> A.   I…figures in books. (Watson 24)

Figures in books. Whatever their function, it is clearly not Coetzee's intention that they correspond with any accuracy to external reality.

BEGINNING – MIDDLE – END
TIME /SPACE
MEMORY

Coetzee's second novel, *From the Heart of the Country*, is even more committed to subverting the game of realism than *Dusklands*. Magda, the protagonist-narrator of the novel, will puzzle a reader seeking plausibility. Her history is obscure:

> The past. I grope around inside my head for the mouth of the tunnel that will lead me back in time and memory past images of myself younger and younger, fresher and fresher, through youth and childhood back to my mother's knee and my origins, but the tunnel is not there. …
>
> But perhaps if I spend a day in the loft emptying old trunks I will find evidence of a credible past. (*HC* 37–38)

This past, like other factual details, is subject to several variations throughout the novel. She has brothers and sisters, or not, for example; her father marries, and she murders him and his new wife. Later, he has not married and is still alive. Magda has no memories, only imagination. "My life is not past, my art cannot be the art of memory," she says (*HC* 43). "I seem never to have been anywhere, I seem to know nothing for sure" (*HC* 17). In other words, she is self-created, or rather, a character in a book, being created by her author as if she is making herself up as she goes along.

Once Magda is seen not as a colonial spinster but as a "figure in a book" with no reliable relationship to external reality, the novel becomes almost like a game, and a comic one at that. The clues are plain once the pattern is recognized: the alternative possibilities in the plot, her desire for her story

> to have a beginning, a middle, and an end…I must not fall asleep in the middle of my life. Out of the blankness that surrounds me I must pluck the incident after incident whose little explosions keep me going. (*HC* 42–43)

Later, she explains, however, that "Lyric is my medium, not chronicle" (*HC* 71). Several times, she alludes to her existence in space rather than time, as would perhaps be characteristic of such a being:

> Perhaps there is no time, perhaps I am deceived when I think of my medium as time, perhaps there is only space, and I a dot

> of light moving erratically from one point in space to another, skipping years in a flash, now a frightened child in the corner of a schoolroom, now an old woman with knobbly fingers, that is also possible, my mind is open, and it would explain some of the tentativeness with which I hold my memories. (*HC* 123–124)

Faced with her father's wounded body, she finds the physical fact of conception

> not possible to believe…If I were told that I am an idea my father had many years ago and then, bored with it, forgot, I would be less incredulous, though still sceptical. I am better explained as an idea I myself had, also many years ago, and have been unable to shake off. (*HC* 69)

Is it possible to hear the author's voice speaking here? In "Realism," the first chapter of *Elizabeth Costello*, the third-person impersonal narrator has this to say:

> Realism has never been comfortable with ideas. It could not be otherwise: realism is premised on the idea that ideas have no autonomous existence, can exist only in things. So when it needs to debate ideas…realism is driven to invent situations—walks in the countryside, conversations—in which characters give voice to contending ideas and thereby in a certain sense embody them. The notion of *embodying* turns out to be pivotal. In such debates ideas do not and indeed cannot float free: they are tied to the speakers by whom they are enounced, and generated from the matrix of individual interests out of which the speakers act in the world. (*EC* 9)

By tying the ideas in this novel to this particular embodiment and writing *From the Heart of the Country* in the first person, what is Coetzee doing? Is he, as Michela Canepari-Labib claims, creating

> novels which oblige readers to question the hierarchies on which our societies are based, and call[ing] upon the entire Western

world and every user of language to question old myths, urging
them to reconsider many of their assumptions and to change the
relations of power [?] (195)

This is rather too much for Coetzee, who resists the idea of producing
"a master narrative for a set of texts that claim to deny all master narratives" (Morphet 464). Certainly, he is subverting the idea of realism in
literature and drawing attention to the role of language in constituting
ideas of reality. As Brian McCaskill argues,

> [I]t is precisely the logic of this stony monologue that finally
> makes it impossible—despite Magda's doubts—to accept her
> words, or Coetzee's writing, as an intransitive and only self-
> referential act of verbal solipsism—as "merely" an instance of
> deconstructive play. Neither "omitted" nor banished to brackets,
> nor yet buried as a deep structure, history in this stony monologue
> has been made to confront its making by language. (462)

Coetzee's playfulness, as always, has a serious purpose, but it is a subtler
purpose than that envisaged by the "baneful readings" characterized by
"reductive allegorising" (McCaskill 469). James Harrison points out that
Magda seeks her identity "among the fears, hopes, evasions, fantasies
and frustrations of her inner life" rather than in the outside world, "and
for that a first-person voice in the present tense seems tailor-made" (82).
As McCaskill argues, Coetzee's purpose is to create a being who seeks
to be "the medium, the median…neither master nor slave, neither parent
nor child, but the bridge between, so that in me the contraries should be
reconciled" (*HC* 133), but who is stalled by the rigid hierarchies of her
linguistic world. Magda creates herself, which must be done in the first
person: the reflexive, middle voice characterizes her very being.

Each of the first-person narrator/protagonists in these two novels is an
entirely isolated being. In fact, is it not the case that most protagonists
are isolated during much of the narrative action in any novel? The kind
of drama which gives rise to narrative usually arises from a solitary individual's struggle against some kind of obstacle, even if the result is rein-
tegration into society at the end of the story, a state Coetzee's characters

rarely achieve. Perhaps the character who comes closest is the Magistrate in *Waiting for the Barbarians.*

The Magistrate describes himself as "a responsible official in the service of the Empire, serving out my days on this lazy frontier, waiting to retire" (*WB* 8). He lives alone but has friends among the townspeople. His period of isolation begins when he fails to ignore the prisoners captured and tortured by the Third Bureau and eventually, in punishment for consorting with a barbarian girl, is imprisoned and tortured himself.

The first paragraph of the novel establishes the Magistrate's resistance to change and sense of superiority to the "new men" like Colonel Joll:

> I have never seen anything like it: two little discs of glass suspended in front of his eyes in loops of wire. Is he blind? I could understand it if he wanted to hide blind eyes. But he is not blind. The discs are dark, they look opaque from the outside, but he can see through them. He tells me they are a new invention. (*WB* 1)

"Signs of a moderate realism," these sunglasses, like Elizabeth Costello's clothes and hair, "[s]upply the particulars, allow the significations to emerge of themselves. A procedure pioneered by Daniel Defoe" (*EC* 4). Moderate realism is a reasonable description of *Waiting for the Barbarians.* The games of *From the Heart of the Country* are left behind for the moment. Magda's status as a figment of her own imagination removes the reader's impulse to identify with her. On the other hand, we are at once recruited on the Magistrate's behalf, and the novel's realism means that we continue to feel sympathy with him throughout his ordeals.

The Magistrate is the most rational of Coetzee's narrators. Pondering his attraction to the barbarian girl, he interrupts himself parenthetically: "(I am not stupid, let me say these things)" (*WB* 64). Realism was not of enough concern to Coetzee for him to set up fictional framing scenarios— a story being told to someone else, or a diary, for example—in these early first-person narratives, which makes this interruption particularly interesting. Whom is he addressing in the imperative here? Who might be imagined as preventing him from speaking (or thinking) these words? Near the end of the novel, he makes an attempt "to set down a record of settlement to be left for posterity buried under the walls of our town" (*WB* 154). He fails, setting down only a "devious…equivocal…reprehensible" message, a plea to set back the clock, a plea for the return of innocence (*WB* 154). This is plainly not the beginning of the novel we have just read: this is not a self-reflexive narrative, supposed, within the fictional frame of the novel, to be written by the narrator. The Magistrate is not a writer, just a narrator, explaining himself to himself and anyone else who might happen to overhear, although there is no likely interlocutor in this fictional world.

After the departure of the soldiers, the Magistrate resumes his former authority, despite the extreme isolation and humiliation he has been subjected to:

> In all measures for our preservation I have taken the lead. No one has challenged me. My beard is trimmed, I wear clean clothes, I have in effect resumed the legal administration that was interrupted a year ago by the arrival of the Civil Guard. (*WB* 145)

He is reintegrated into society, but much has changed: he often finds himself "feeling stupid, like a man who lost his way long ago but presses on along a road that may lead nowhere" (*WB* 156).

In a 1985 interview, Coetzee was asked about the ambiguities in his novels, especially *Waiting for the Barbarians*:

> Q. I kept asking myself, for example, who's the Barbarian here? And what can this mean, and all sorts of questions, and this is something I like very much about your works: it forces the reader into a very personal reflection, but through the telling of a story. … I suppose that this is one of your main purposes. Am I right there, or wrong?
>
> A. No, you're not wrong. People ask me whether I feel any rupture between my life as an academic and my life as a writer and the answer is: no. And part of the reason why the answer is no is that I believe very strongly in the critical activity of the literary critic—and I hope that I bring across in my fiction writing some of that same concern with the importance of criticism which is to me a matter of taking nothing for granted. Everything is capable of being questioned. (Sévry 6)

This skepticism, as I mentioned in chapter 2, is bound up with Coetzee's resistance to political or social certitudes. But although there is not an easily identified, "unquestioned" message in *Waiting for the Barbarians*, it would be perverse to deny the political implications of the novel, and its straightforward approach to realism is best suited to Coetzee's purpose: no parody or language games but a sober tale related by a sober, civilized man whose point of view the reader can largely understand and share.

Realism and politics again make an alliance in *Life & Times of Michael K*. Talking about the "realism" of this novel, he pointed out that its geography, though based in the "real" South Africa, is not "trustworthy,"

> because I don't have much interest in, or can't seriously engage myself with, the kind of realism that takes pride in copying the "real world." The option was, of course, open to me to invent a world out of place and time and situate the action there, as I did in *Waiting for the Barbarians*; but that side of *Waiting for the Barbarians* was an immense labor, and what would have been the point, this time round? (Morphet 455)

Life & Times of Michael K is the first of Coetzee's novels written mostly in the third person. I do not believe that there is always a watertight connection between point of view and identification: the reader is not automatically more tightly bound to a first-person narrator than to a focalizing character whose actions are described by a third-person narrator. However, in this case, this is the effect, and probably the intention, of Coetzee's choice of the third person for Michael K's story. For one thing, a third-person narrator has more freedom to move between points of view, and in fact, there are three in the early pages of the novel. First, there is the midwife. Then Anna K's view predominates, and then, in the middle of a paragraph on page 8, the focus passes finally from Anna to her son Michael:

> She expected Michael to ask how she could believe that a small country town would take to its bosom two strangers, one of them an old woman in bad health. She had even prepared an answer. But not for an instant did Michael doubt her. (*MK* 8)

As soon as Michael's point of view takes over in that last sentence, he also takes over the active role in the story. As Anna passes on her dream of returning to Prince Albert, the town where she was born, Michael immediately begins to act to try to bring it about, and Anna becomes passive. Michael takes on the impossible task of arranging to transport himself and his sick mother out of the city to a distant town, through a country at war with itself: this is South Africa as it might have been if civil war had broken out in the 1980s.

Michael does not have a strongly developed sense of himself. Encountering a stranger, "he saw a man younger than himself wearing a green and gold track suit and carrying a wooden tool-chest. What the stranger saw he did not know" (*MK* 47). It is not clear whether this lack of knowledge is conscious, but later, meeting someone else, Michael thinks, "He thinks I am truly an idiot" (*MK* 62). This is the thought of someone who has an idea of himself as other than an idiot. However, he is not able to fathom himself completely:

> Always, when he tried to explain himself to himself, there remained a gap, a hole, a darkness before which his understanding baulked, into which it was useless to pour words. The words were eaten up, the gap remained. His was always a story with a hole in it: a wrong story, always wrong. (*MK* 110)

This is an admission of failure that does Michael no discredit; it is not so different from the Magistrate's failures of self-analysis in *Waiting for the Barbarians*. It is linked with his decision not to join the rebels, that decision which Nadine Gordimer found so controversial but which makes Michael a Coetzee character, a resister. However, Michael does not have the high intellect of the Magistrate, and to introduce an intellectual element into the novel, Coetzee has to introduce another point of view.

Part 2 of the novel is narrated by the medical officer in a retraining camp in Cape Town where Michael has been sent, accused of "running a staging post for guerrillas" (*MK* 129). The medical officer—he is not a doctor but a pharmacist—gets Michael's name wrong, or rather, accepts the official version, that his name is Michaels. This is only the beginning of his failure to comprehend Michael, though he trains the full force of his intellect on the problem. At first, he thinks of him as an idiot, but at the end of part 2, the medical officer imagines himself chasing the escaping Michael, pleading with and berating him:

> At first I thought of you, I will confess, as a figure of fun. I did indeed urge Major van Rensburg to exempt you from the camp regime, but only because I thought that putting you through the motions of rehabilitation would be like trying to teach a rat or a mouse or (dare I say it?) a lizard to bark and beg and catch a ball. As time passed, however, I slowly began to see the originality of the resistance you offered. You were not a hero and did not pretend to be, not even a hero of fasting. ... You tried sincerely, I believe, to do as you were told. ... Then as I watched you day after day I slowly began to understand the truth: that you were crying secretly, unknown to your conscious self (forgive the term), for a different kind of food, food that no camp could supply. (*MK* 163)

As Michael draws away from him, he shouts (or imagines he would shout) after him, "Have I understood you? If I am right, hold up your right hand; if I am wrong, hold up your left!" (*MK* 167). Here we leave the medical officer, absurdly stranded, still unable to solve the riddle of Michael, although certain that there is a solution, "that Michaels means something, and the meaning he has is not private to me" (*MK* 165), and imagining himself into this ridiculous, humiliating position in his desire to pin down that meaning.

Part 3 is a short coda, once again in the third person, focalized through Michael. It is almost a relief to be back in the simple realm of Michael's consciousness after the medical officer's compulsive quest for significance. He tells his story to some people who befriend him, but "it struck him...that his story was paltry, not worth the telling, full of the same old gaps that he would never learn how to bridge" (*MK* 176).

But Michael's story *is* worth the telling. It has occupied the past 176 pages. We laugh at the contortions of the medical officer's attempts to wrest a meaning from Michael, but we are in his shoes, as readers, trying to interpret Michael's life and times as an allegory of modern South

African politics, or as a Kafkaesque dream, or whatever particular solution fits our cast of mind or the current literary fashion.

> At least, he thought, at least I have not been clever, and come back to Sea Point full of stories…I was mute and stupid in the beginning, I will be mute and stupid at the end. There is nothing to be ashamed of in being simple. (*MK* 182)

A fairly sophisticated train of thought for a simple mind: Michael K might not understand everything, but he has somehow survived on his own terms and in the end produces an image of continued survival, on water drawn from an abandoned well with a bent teaspoon. It is a ludicrous image, but Michael's survival has always verged on the incredible. The temptation is strong to assign a large significance to it: the survival of the spirit of freedom in the face of overwhelming odds, for example.

and so?

* * * * *

With *Foe*, we are back with the first person again. From the beginning, the narrative is enclosed in quotation marks, so someone is speaking or writing; someone female, with long hair, clad in a petticoat. Four pages in, we encounter the second person to whom this is addressed, in an aside, "the stranger (who was of course the Cruso I told you of)" (*F* 9), although we are still unaware of the identity of this person. It is not until page 45 that the narrator, whom we now know from her explanation to Cruso is Susan Barton (*F* 10), addresses "Mr Foe" by name, and on the next page, at the beginning of part 2, we are told what it is we have been reading:

> I have set down the history of our time on the island as well as I can, and enclose it herewith. It is a sorry limping affair (the history, not the time itself)—"the next day," its refrain goes, "the next day…the next day"—but you will know how to set it right. (*F* 47)

Part 2 consists of a series of letters from Susan Barton to Mr. Foe, still in inverted commas; it is not until part 3 that the narrative becomes direct and unmediated. Even then, however, much is reported conversation. In the five pages of the final section, part 4, the "I" has changed: although this narrator is unnamed and unidentified—Coetzee himself disclaims knowledge of who it is (Scott 99)—his discovery of the bodies of Susan and Foe makes it clear this is a new voice. He tries once to speak, "[b]ut this is not a place of words" (*F* 157).

Most of the words in *Foe* come from Susan Barton as writer or speaker. The novel is in many ways like *From the Heart of the Country* in its questioning of reality and the role of self-creation in fiction:

> I presented myself to you in words I knew to be my own…and for a long time afterwards, when I was writing those letters that were never read by you, and were later not sent, and at last not even written down, I continued to trust in my own authorship.
>
> Yet, in the same room as yourself at last, where I need surely not relate to you my every action…I continue to describe and explain. … Why do I speak, to whom do I speak, when there is no need to speak?
>
> In the beginning I thought I would tell you the story of the island and, being done with that, return to my former life. But now all my life grows to be story and there is nothing of my own left to me. (*F* 133)

Foe's response to her, from the standpoint of the experienced writer, harks back again to *From the Heart of the Country* and foreshadows the enigmatic position of the protagonist of *Slow Man*:

> [A]s to who among us is a ghost and who not I have nothing to say: it is a question we can only stare at in silence, like a bird before a snake, hoping it will not swallow us.
>
> But if you cannot rid yourself of your doubts, I have something to say that may be of comfort. Let us confront our worst fear, which is that we have all of us been called into the world from a different order (which we have now forgotten) by a conjurer unknown to us. … Then I ask nevertheless: Have we thereby lost our freedom?…You and I know, in our different ways, how rambling an occupation writing is; and conjuring is surely much the same. (*F* 134–135)

Perhaps the new voice in part 4, which knows all about Susan and Foe and Friday, is that of the unknown conjurer, though he has conjured more than the cloud-pictures Foe speaks of (*F* 135); the dead bodies he finds are substantial, though not realistic: their skin is "dry as paper" and their bodies "quietly composed, he in a nightshirt, she in her shift. There is even a faint smell of lilac" (*F* 153). And the wordless realm he enters, "the home of Friday," is entered through reading the words of Susan's manuscript, the words beginning the novel, "At last I could row no further. ... With a sigh, making barely a splash, I slip overboard " (*F* 155).

and so?

Inhabiting the female sensibility seems to suit Coetzee well as a writer. Of his eleven novels, four have female protagonists, and three of these are narrated in the first person, whereas only three of the six first-person novels have male narrators for the most part; even then, in *Diary of a Bad Year*, Anya's narrative is included as well as J. C.'s. In Susan's case, it is perhaps partly a matter of practicality that determined her sex. If Coetzee needed someone to get close to Cruso, and subsequently to Foe, a woman is a more likely candidate than another man. In his interview with Tony Morphet, he says,

> my interest clearly lies with Foe's foe, the *unsuccessful* author—worse, authoress—Susan Barton[.] How can one question power ("success") from a position of power? One ought to question it from its antagonist position, namely, the position of weakness. (Morphet 462)

The females in *From the Heart of the Country* and *Foe* are marginal, but not more so than many of Coetzee's male characters. Susan says to Foe, "I am a free woman who asserts her freedom by telling her story according to her own desire" (*F* 131): hardly the words of a downtrodden victim. However, as she anticipates, she is left out of Foe's published account. Morphet asks him about his "position as a successful author" and draws an extraordinarily aggressive response, particularly considering that he is attempting to distance himself from an exercise of power: "In this interview, I am being installed in a position of power—power, in this case, over my own text." But how does this relate to his statement, a few moments before, that "What you call 'the nature and processes of fiction' may also be called the question of *who writes*? Who takes up the position of power, pen in hand?" Clearly, the answer is Coetzee, even though he is inhabiting Susan's point of view, but he uses this power to endow Susan with the power that Foe denies her: Coetzee has created her especially for that purpose. Nevertheless, he says,

> I would hate to say either that there is a feminist point or that I *chose* the narrator. The narrator chose me. There is a flippant way of saying that, and a serious way. The book deals with choosing in the serious sense. (Morphet 462)

Age of Iron, Coetzee's sixth novel, is the last for some time to be narrated in the first person, once again by a female. Elizabeth Curren is a strong-minded, liberal woman, a former academic, with a house of her own. Her position in white society is secure. It is in the world of her servant and her servant's family that she is irrelevant. Like *Foe*, it has the type of narrative scenario that is absent from the first four novels, and, even more plainly than Foe, from the very first page it is addressed to a second person, the absent adult daughter of an elderly, sick woman. "Home truths, a mother's truth: from now to the end that is all you will hear from me" (*AI* 15), she writes. This letter is unrequited and designedly so: it is not to be sent until the writer is dead:

> These papers, these words that either you read *now* or else you will never read. Will they reach you? Have they reached you? Two ways of asking the same question, a question to which I will never know the answer, never. To me this letter will forever be words committed to the waves: a message in a bottle with the stamps of the Republic of South Africa on it, and your name. (*AI* 32)

Elizabeth Curren is well aware of the distortions of subjectivity in her narrative:

> I tell you the story of this morning mindful that the story-teller, from her office, claims the place of right. It is through my eyes that you see; the voice that speaks in your head is mine. ...

> Now, my child, flesh of my flesh, my best self, I ask you to draw
> back. I tell you this story not so that you will feel for me but so that
> you will learn how things are. ... So I ask you: attend to the writing,
> not to me. If lies and pleas and excuses weave among the words,
> listen for them. Do not pass them over, do not forgive them easily.
> Read all, even this adjuration, with a cold eye. (*AI* 103–104)

Directly addressed to the fictional reader, this has the force of an appeal
from the actual author to the actual reader: beware of my complicity,
whether or not it be intentional. Nevertheless, *Age of Iron* is a work
of sober realism, like *Waiting for the Barbarians* and *Life & Times of
Michael K*, without the more obvious metafictional overtones of *From
the Heart of the Country* and *Foe*. The realism is reinforced by the occasional reference to the physical act of writing. "His voice startled me
as I sat in the kitchen writing" (*F* 142); "I was sitting up in bed, gloves
on my hands, the writing pad on my knees" (*F* 174). Only the ending
requires sleight of hand: the death scene is always a difficulty in the first-
person novel. Even Vercueil, the homeless man who seems to figure as
the angel of death, is realistic, with his dirty fingernails and his repulsive
cooking. In this respect, Coetzee cautioned an interviewer, "remember
that the book is narrated through one person alone; all perceptions are
her perceptions" (Viola 7). As Derek Attridge says,

> [I]nterpretations of Vercueil...that allegorize him as the angel
> of death must take account of Mrs Curren's own tendency to do
> just that throughout the novel—as well as her readiness to reject
> the allegory at other times. At the very least, we have to say that
> an allegorical reading of Vercueil's part in the novel cannot be
> straightforward. ("Against Allegory" 64)

Despite his resistance to political pressures, it seems that Coetzee has
tended to confine his more extreme experiments with deconstruction to
the novels that have less direct bearing on the politics of settler societies.
As Dominic Head writes,

> It is true that all along Coetzee has betrayed a dynamic of resis-
> tance that challenges the dominance of the political over the

literary; but it is equally true that his work up to and including *The Master of Petersburg*...acknowledges the power of contemporary politics to delimit any fictional project. ("Belief" 100)

The Master of Petersburg starts firmly anchored in a place and time: "October 1869. A droshky passes slowly down a street in the Haymarket district of St Petersburg" (*MP* 1). However, the ideal (though improbable) reader who has come to this book without having read the blurb or anything else about the novel will not know until page 33 the identity of the "man in late middle age, bearded and stooped, with a high forehead and heavy eyebrows" who alights from the droshky (*MP* 1).

Coetzee's imagining of a few months in the life of Dostoevsky "when he was struggling with the composition of a book, not knowing what it was going to be about, just knowing it had to be a big book" (Scott 99) once again raises the question of "who takes up the position of power, pen in hand" (Morphet 462). *The Master of Petersburg* is narrated in a somewhat Dostoevskian third person. The opening bears a family resemblance to the beginning of *Crime and Punishment*, published in 1866, for example, though not to the first-person narrative of *Demons*, the book that Dostoevsky was struggling with at the time *The Master of Petersburg* is set. However, before the first page is over, the point of view has passed to the character "Dostoevsky" (whom I will henceforth call "Fyodor"), through whose senses the rest of the book is mediated: though the third-person voice continues, we never again see him from the outside, wearing "a dark suit of somewhat démodé cut" (*MP* 1), as he appears in the fourth paragraph of the book. The narrative effectively passes into free indirect style: though technically, the third person is used, the words, emotions, and ideas belong to the character rather than the narrator or the implied author.

The parallels between *The Master of Petersburg* and Dostoevsky's work are many—metafictional use of names, echoes of situations, and other details which float about in Fyodor's subconscious and occasionally surface as jokes—and these have been elucidated by several commentators.[1] The final chapter, titled "Stavrogin," shows Fyodor at last managing to write, and in doing so, producing two stories designed as "an assault upon the innocence of a child. … To corrupt a child is to force God. The device he has made arches and springs shut like a trap, a trap to catch God" (*MP* 249). Dostoevsky's character Stavrogin, in the chapter "At Tikhon's," omitted from *Demons*, confesses to physically corrupting a child. Here, in a perverse demonstration of the power of narrative, Coetzee's Fyodor corrupts a child of the same name, Matryona, merely through writing. The power that the writer has is the power of betrayal, leading to "a life without honour; treachery without limit; confession without end" (*MP* 222). No wonder Coetzee is loath in his interview with Morphet to be "installed in a position of power," seeing "'successful author' [as] a…highly barbed phrase" (Morphet 462). However, in *The Master of Petersburg*, he cannot claim to be identifying himself with the position of weakness, from where he says "one ought to question" power (Morphet 462). Fyodor, despite his troubles, cannot divorce himself from the position of "successful author" but realizes that to achieve that success, "he had to give up his soul in return" (*MP* 250). Is it open to Coetzee to claim a distance from his powerful writer/character Fyodor while claiming kinship with his powerless writer/character Susan Barton? With *The Master of Petersburg*, we are surely back with the kind of questions of complicity arising in *Dusklands*.

Coetzee's next three books all begin with sentences whose subject is a third-person pronoun. *Boyhood* and *Youth*, Coetzee's first two volumes of memoirs, like *Master of Petersburg*, only reveal the name of their protagonist—a name shared, of course, by the author—some way into the text. The third-person narrative, and Coetzee's reluctance to identify himself as the subject of these memoirs, probably springs partly from his sense that autobiography is constructed in retrospect and therefore unreliable. Joanna Scott's interview with Coetzee was published in 1997, and it presumably took place before the publication of *Boyhood* in the same year, since she doesn't mention the book. However, given the timing of the interview, it is likely to have taken place either during or soon after the book's composition, although he doesn't volunteer the fact, and the idea of an autobiographical project was clearly in his mind:

> I could have no idea of an alternative to the environment in which I lived, so what impressions I had can't, logically speaking, count as impressions of this country. They were just impressions of life. And by now they have been recalled, revisited, revised so often that I can hardly claim with any confidence that they belong to my childhood. They belong, now, to the childhood I have constructed for myself in retrospect, that is, to autobiography. (Scott 82–83)

In *Boyhood*, especially, there are signs that the point of view, which purports to be tied to the consciousness of a child, is in fact contaminated by the writing adult. The child's conflicting feelings towards his parents, for example, are explained with a clarity that one would not expect in a ten-year-old child:

> He puts the blame on his mother for not beating him. At the same time that he is glad he wears shoes and takes out books from the public library and stays away from school when he has a cold—all the things that set him apart—he is angry with his mother for not having normal children and making them live a normal life... . He is angry with his mother for turning him into something unnatural, something that needs to be protected if it is to continue to live. (*B* 7–8)

Youth uses irony as a distancing device more than *Boyhood* does, the young John revealing his naïve attitudes and prejudices by his relentless self-questioning, but occasionally we can see his questions broadening out to a point of view which might also belong to his namesake, the author Coetzee. This impression might be encouraged by the transition to the first person in a paragraph like this:

> *The life of the mind*, he thinks to himself: is that what we have dedicated ourselves to, I and these other lonely wanderers in the bowels of the British Museum? Will there be a reward for us one day? Will our solitariness lift, or is the life of the mind its own reward? (*Y* 55)

Between these two memoirs comes *Disgrace*, published in 1999. What distinguishes it from the two parts of the autobiographical project that surrounds it is more the structure and shape than the voice, at least at first. The third-person pronoun is the subject of the first sentence, again, with information about this "he" introduced bit by bit. Although it is clearly the voice of an older man, surer of himself and his opinions, the narrative is still full of questions, few of which are answered with any clarity. And the language of his self-assessments often seems to chime with that of John in *Youth*, although without the ironic gap between author and character. David Lurie thinks of himself as "[n]ot a bad man but not good either. Not cold but not hot, even at his hottest. ... Lacking in fire. Will that be the verdict on him, the verdict of the universe and its all-seeing eye?" (*D* 195). In the same vein, John, in *Youth*, thinks, "If he were a warmer person he would no doubt find it all easier: life, love, poetry. But warmth is not in his nature" (*Y* 168).

It is tempting to think that Coetzee is making a point about the inadequacy of academic criticism when, after a lifetime as a literary scholar, Lurie is surprised by the vagaries of the creative process: he finds that the sound of the piano is "too rounded, too physical, too rich" for the chamber opera, *Byron in Italy*, that he is writing, and an old toy banjo of Lucy's suits his purposes better. "So this is art, he thinks, and this is how it does its work! How strange! How fascinating!" (*D* 184). Nevertheless, Lurie realizes that his opera is no masterpiece and may never be finished: "The lyric impulse in him may not be dead, but after decades of starvation it can crawl forth from its cave only pinched, stunted, deformed" (*D* 214). But Lurie has been creating the story of his life all along. The first chapter is a complacent hymn of self-regard, although "he has not forgotten the last chorus of *Oedipus*: Call no man happy until he is dead" (*D* 2). Lucy tries to jolt him out of his solipsism:

> You behave as if everything I do is part of the story of your life. You are the main character, I am a minor character who doesn't make an appearance until halfway through. Well, contrary to what

> you think, people are not divided into major and minor. I am not
> minor. (*D* 198)

It is not clear that he takes her point. This section ends with his tears at
being "[a] father without the sense to have a son: is this how it is all going
to end, is this how his line is going to run out, like water dribbling into
the earth?" (*D* 199). By the end of the book, he has certainly advanced
some way from the smug beginning: "One gets used to things getting
harder; one ceases to be surprised that what used to be as hard as hard
can be grows harder yet" (*D* 219). And he gives up the crippled dog that
has become almost a pet to Bev Shaw's exterminating needle, because
the "time must come, it cannot be evaded" (*D* 219). This ending leaves
questions unanswered. Why should he not adopt the dog and let it live,
this dog that "would die for him, he knows" (*D* 215)? Is it a noble gesture
of renunciation to destroy the only being that loves him unconditionally?
Surely this is sacrificing the dog to some entirely human sense of a higher
purpose? One imagines that Elizabeth Costello would not approve.

Elizabeth Costello must be unique in the annals of fiction: a novel
consisting of eight "lessons," most of which have been delivered as
public lectures or conference papers and, indeed, published before
in various forms. Many critics have recounted having heard, to their
surprise, one of these lessons when they were expecting a more conventional academic paper from Coetzee. I myself was present at the
ACLALS (Association for Commonwealth Literature and Language
Studies) conference in Canberra in 2001 when he presented lesson 5,
"The Humanities in Africa." Many critics have assumed that Coetzee's
"impersonation" of Costello makes a feminist point about how a woman's point of view on, say, animal rights, is regarded as less valid than
a man's. It seems odd, however, to choose quite such a woman for this
purpose: a world-famous author being awarded a major literary prize,
as Costello is in lessons 3 and 4, is not in a typical subaltern position.
Laura Wright, writing about *The Lives of Animals* (1999), which com-
prises lessons 3 and 4 in an earlier form, discusses the way critics have
treated Elizabeth Costello's relationship with Coetzee, some simply

conflating them, others "overdetermin[ing] the distance" ("Feminist-Vegetarian" 197):

> The third-person narrated *Disgrace* (1999), the novel that not inci-
> dentally followed the publication of *The Lives of Animals*, poses an
> interesting counterpoint because although both Coetzee and protag-
> onist David Lurie are male and both teach university-level litera-
> ture, critics do not concern themselves with setting up a distinction
> between these two; we seem to more readily accept that Coetzee
> and Lurie are distinct persons, and the "laws" that govern readings
> of fiction forbid us from doing something as reductive as conflating
> the positions of author and protagonist. But it seems more probable
> that such an option is never considered because Coetzee does not
> perform Lurie in the way that he performs Costello. ... [I]t seems
> that a productive way of examining Elizabeth Costello is to posit
> her as the imagined body through which Coetzee enacts emotional
> speech, even as he examines the limitations of such sympathetic
> embodiment. ("Feminist-Vegetarian" 199)

In this reading, Costello was created specifically for the purpose of being *spoken* by Coetzee. He has no difficulty *writing* emotional speech through his male protagonists. However, at the same conference where he read lesson 5, he gave a reading from *Youth*, where the young John Coetzee was heard voicing emotions: in what way is this different? Perhaps it is merely determined by the expectations of the audience: the Elizabeth Costello piece was advertised in the program as a paper on "The Humanities in Africa," while the reading from *Youth* was billed as a reading from a work in progress.

Can *Elizabeth Costello* be read in the same way a novel is read, or is it indeed just a book of essays? Costello the aging Australian writer retains enough individuality to be a convincing character, even though she could be seen as a convenient vessel for Coetzee's purposes, a little like Gulliver was for Swift. However, as Jennifer Szalai points out, *Elizabeth Costello*

> is a remarkable complement to Coetzee's previous work. It is
> a story that reveals the possibilities of storytelling through the

> peregrinations of an aging novelist constantly confronted by her
> obstinate body and meddling intellect. ... Most of *Elizabeth
> Costello* is...made up of stories that were told in lieu of lectures,
> and it is Costello's life, not just the dithering content of her aca-
> demic addresses, that compose [*sic*] the truth of these fictions. (85)

In lesson 1, "Realism," Coetzee alerts the reader to the conventions of
narrative that are usually hidden:

> It is not a good idea to interrupt the narrative too often, since sto-
> rytelling works by lulling the reader or listener into a dreamlike
> state in which the time and space of the real world fade away,
> superseded by the time and space of the fiction. Breaking into
> the dream draws attention to the constructedness of the story,
> and plays havoc with the realist illusion. However, unless certain
> scenes are skipped over we will be here all afternoon. (*EC* 16)

We meet Costello's son John Bernard, divorced, a lecturer in physics
and astronomy in Massachusetts, who is taking a year off and for some
reason, although his mother lives in Melbourne, tells the woman he has
just slept with that his watch is on Canberra time (*EC* 27). Why Canberra time? Canberra time is the same as Melbourne time: is he living
in Canberra for this year he is having off, or does he say Canberra time
just because Canberra is the capital of Australia? A small puzzle, hardly
worth a moment's thought. But then we meet John again in lessons 3
and 4, when Costello visits him in Massachusetts two years later, and he
has acquired a wife, whom "he met and married...while they were both
graduate students at Johns Hopkins" (*EC* 61), and two sons. Clearly, the
wife is required for this part of the narrative, where she would have been
in the way in the earlier part. Coetzee is showing us as clearly as he can
that the conventions of realism are of little importance.

Formally, the whole book is in the third person. Lessons 1, 3, and 4 are,
however, focalized through Costello's son John, while the others are all
seen through Costello's own point of view. Thus, we see an aging woman
from the perspective of her son, who admires her and takes pride in her
achievements but at the same time feels both protective and exasperated

and is glad to see her go so his family life can regain equilibrium, but we also see the same woman from her own viewpoint, living through various adventures, including the final, though inconclusive one, "At the Gate." There are, of course, long passages in the first person throughout the book, when Costello is speaking before an audience, and sometimes when other characters—the Nigerian writer Emmanuel Egudu in lesson 2, and Costello's sister Blanche in lesson 5—are similarly addressing various gatherings. But at the end of lesson 5, there is a coda that, as far as I recall, Coetzee did not read at the conference I attended. Elizabeth Costello writes a letter to her sister about her visits to an elderly man in a nursing home years before. During these visits, she relates, she posed bare-breasted for Mr. Phillips, who had been a painter. In her discussion of this "act of humanity," she appeals to her sister Blanche, a Catholic nun of antihumanist sentiments: "Surely from Zululand, where you have such an abundance of unclothed bodies to gaze on, you must concede, Blanche, that there is nothing more humanly beautiful than a woman's breasts" (*EC* 150). This jars when it is considered as coming from a man writing in a woman's voice. I'm not sure that all women would concede such a thing: many might, but possibly fewer women than men. Is Coetzee allowing his heterosexual masculinity to intrude into this conversation between elderly sisters? Is he deliberately drawing attention to his narrative cross-dressing as a distancing device?

Talking about *Foe* in his interview with Morphet, Coetzee said, "The narrator chose me. There is a flippant way of saying that, and a serious way. The book deals with choosing in the serious sense" (Morphet 462). I would hesitate to call *Slow Man*, the novel in which Elizabeth Costello appears as an author trying to interfere in the life of her character, a flippant novel. However, it is surely not entirely serious, and is possibly his least serious book of all.

Elizabeth Costello insists that Paul Rayment came to her, rather than the opposite: "You came to me, that is all I can say. You occurred to me—a man with a bad leg and no future and an unsuitable passion" (*SM* 85). Paul never comes to understand what she means, and perhaps the reader will never quite grasp it either. Behaving cautiously, refusing to act to seduce Marijana, he refuses to play the part of a character in a novel who sets the action of the story in train by imprudence. How often, reading a narrative, one thinks, if only X had not made that foolish decision, he would have saved himself from much trouble and pain—but then there would be no plot, no story. *Slow Man* in this way is a kind of antinovel. Since the point of view remains with Paul Rayment (in the third person), it is possible to read *Slow Man* as a dramatization not only of a character's view of a writer, but of a lifetime of critics and readers asking Coetzee unanswerable questions about the nature of the creative process, as so often demonstrated in interviews: trying to pin down exactly what happens when, how and why certain characters were chosen and created. In one of her more candid moments, Costello responds to Rayment's question, "Why pour all this effort into me?" (*SM* 154):

> Of course I have asked myself that, Paul. Many times. And of course, by some standards, you are a small fish. The question is, by what standards? The question is, how small? Patience, I tell myself: perhaps there is something yet to be squeezed out of him, like a last drop of juice out of a lemon, or like blood out of a stone. But yes, you may be right, you may indeed be a mistake, I will concede that. If you were not a mistake I would probably not still be here in Adelaide. I stay on because I don't know what to do about you. (*SM* 155)

There is an echo here of something Coetzee said to Scott, when she asked him, "Is there a point when you know something is a viable project?" He responded,

> Yes, there is: when I've invested so much time in it that I can't afford to stop, can't afford to face the fact that I've wasted six months of my life, or whatever. So I soldier on, and the book gets written. (Scott 95)

Coetzee is also perhaps playing with another idea he expressed in his interview with Scott: "I remember feeling a lot of affection for Susan Barton, by the end, and wondering why I never got to meet her. What people call confusing the real and the imaginary" (Scott 99). Why not introduce a character to an author in the same fictional milieu? Of course, this is not a new idea: Italo Calvino and Luigi Pirandello were playing such games decades ago. And perhaps putting Elizabeth Costello in a fiction about someone else, where she does not seem to belong, where, she says, "the moment you decide to take charge I will fade away" (*SM* 100), is, since he is no doubt aware of the critical propensity to conflate him with Costello, demonstrating that real and imaginary are perhaps extremes on a continuum rather than absolute opposites.

It hardly seems necessary to mention that the realism of the setting in Adelaide is not exact. The background is no more than sketched in, anyway, but small details niggle away at the sense of place for someone who lives in the city and knows it well. Magill Road is a very odd choice of shopping destination for someone, especially a cyclist, living in North Adelaide, for example, and none of the pedal boats on the Torrens River is shaped like a swan (*SM* 154). No doubt residents of other places in which Coetzee's novels are set would be able to produce similar examples. But these place names and details are not intended to reflect a preexisting reality but to provide "signs of a moderate realism" from which the "significations [may] emerge of themselves" (*EC* 4). So why bother with realism at all? As the narrator says in *Elizabeth Costello*, "The notion of *embodying* turns out to be pivotal" (*EC* 9). Using realistic scenarios, which need only to be lightly sketched—the details do not need to be laboriously researched and reproduced—*requires* that the ideas are embodied. But it also *allows* ideas to become embodied. The view from nowhere that philosophers have aspired to is, in realistic fiction, an impossibility, and this merely underlines the fact that it is also an impossibility in "real life." As Coetzee said to Scott,

> Novels engage with particularities. From a certain distance Michael K and Elizabeth Curren may both be seen as responding to what you call violence. But in fact they are two people at different moments in history acting out of complexes of pressures and desires that are quite individual and which set them far apart. My fidelity is ultimately to them and for their unique plights, not to any grand historical trajectory they may be seen as belonging to. (Scott 101)

I am not sure what significance can be read into Coetzee's two-decade-long retreat from first person: he did not write a novel which is formally in the first person between *Foe* in 1986 and *Diary of a Bad Year* in 2007, although of course there have been long passages of first-person discourse within several of the intervening novels. The third person theoretically has the freedom denied to a first-person narrator, to move between points of view, but Coetzee rarely does this and usually uses a generalized form of free indirect style. The point of view in *Disgrace* is that of David Lurie, and in *Slow Man*, it is Paul Rayment's, and after the very first page of *The Master of Petersburg*, we are confined to Fyodor's focalizing consciousness. Many critics point out the effect of the third-person narrative in *Boyhood* and *Youth*, "a device that serves to alienate the author from a self he reluctantly claims as his own while simultaneously disrupting our notion of authorial and narratorial verisimilitude in the realm of autobiography," according to Wright ("Feminist-Vegetarian" 198). In that case, it is true that the third person contributes to the distance between the author and the constructed "character" of his younger self. However, if the only reason for using the third person were to claim a difference from his characters, then logically, the first person would be the best way to claim some common identity, and, despite the importance Coetzee attaches to admitting complicity, I do not believe he is trying to claim a common identity with either Eugene Dawn or Jacobus Coetzee in *Dusklands* by using the first person. Furthermore, he can use either voice to create characters with whom the reader identifies closely, and he can create distance using either voice as well. After all, do we not know Michael K more intimately than the medical officer in *Life & Times of Michael*, despite the usual assumptions about point of view? Much depends on the moment by moment, word by word effects of the narrative, as demonstrated by Derek Attridge in his article "Against Allegory": the "intellectual, affective, and physical" events "that may occur in an engaged reading" (70). The transitions in a passage between third person and first person, for example, the complexity of thought expressed by a character which might broaden sometimes into something which is more likely to be an author's thought: these are all aspects of the point of view of a novel which cannot be encompassed in simple categories of narrative person.

It is significant that it is quite unusual for Coetzee to dramatize more than one point of view in his novels. *Elizabeth Costello* includes parts focalized through her son, *Life & Times of Michael K* has the section narrated by the medical officer, but otherwise, Coetzee's novels, until *Diary of a Bad Year*, have been tightly focused and focalized through a single point of view. *Diary of a Bad Year* formally contains two first-person points of view, but there are gradations within and interplay between those voices. Three narratives share the pages of this book. The upper part of each page, usually one-half to two-thirds, is taken up in part 1 with the "Strong Opinions" of the writer, who, we discover by reading the narrative underneath, is an elderly South African author with the initials J. C. who now lives in Australia. Starting on page 23, another narrative runs along the bottom of each page. The narrator here is Anya, a young woman who lives in the same block of high-rise apartments as J. C. and who agrees to type his manuscript. Part 2 continues with the same formal arrangement, but the "opinions" have mellowed and broadened under Anya's influence. But even this is not the whole picture. In part 2, J. C.'s narrative, after twenty pages, consists of a letter from Anya, while her narrative is interrupted by a long diatribe from her boyfriend Alan, reported by her with her commentary. The final five pages contain the last two of J. C.'s "soft opinions," Anya's letter to him, and her own narrative voice. The book has begun with the rhetoric of the writer juxtaposed with his "behind-the-scenes" personal narrative: the same source, but two outlets, one formal and public, the other informal and private. At the end of the book, the informal part of his narrative has been displaced by Anya's letter. Thus, although the book begins with a preponderance of J. C.'s voice, when it finishes, his narrative has given way to Anya's, as if the death with which he is so preoccupied has taken place, silencing his informal voice but leaving his formal, written prose to survive him.

The informal narrative often explicitly refers to the formal one. As the book progresses, we also begin to see some influence the other way, for example, when he remarks towards the end of part 1, in "On English

Usage," that "I survey my elderly coevals and see all too many consumed with grouchiness" (*DBY* 121), and the second diary is made up of the "second, gentler set of opinions" he writes under Anya's influence, as we discover from his narrative (*DBY* 119).

The temptation to conflate J. C. with J. M. Coetzee is strong and encouraged in various ways. J. C. is a South African author who has written a novel called *Waiting for the Barbarians*. He has recently moved to Australia. However, in many other ways, Coetzee distinguishes himself from his character. J. C. is about seven years older than Coetzee; he lives alone in Sydney, rather than a thousand miles away in Adelaide with a long-term partner; he has had no children, whereas Coetzee had two, one of whom died in 1989. The opinions J. C. expresses must therefore be regarded as part of the fiction—the pronouncements of someone like Coetzee, but not actually Coetzee himself. James Wood writes,

> We are warned that it is naïve to confuse author and character, even when—especially when—that character is also a novelist. But if Coetzee's novels deflect such inquiries, they also invite them, not least because of the provoking extremity, even irrationality, of their ideas. ... His books make all the right postmodern noises, but their energy lies in their besotted relationship to an older, Dostoyevskian tradition, in which we feel the desperate impress of the confessing author, however recessed and veiled. ("Squall Lines" 140)

Coetzee is playing a tricky game here: given that critics have routinely conflated him with his character Elizabeth Costello, with whom he has relatively little in common, it seems deliberately provocative for him to present a character even more like himself to voice these sometimes controversial opinions, thus owning them and disowning them at the same time. The combination of the embodiment of these opinions in an aging, ailing body and the staging of their composition in a narrative that is clearly fictional encourages the reader's skepticism as to their status as beliefs sincerely held by the author. At the same time, their inclusion in this novel, with its varied points of view and registers of prose, encourages the reader to ponder the source of all such statements which, however magisterial in their effect, can only emanate from a fallible human source.

How fallible that human might be is rehearsed in the next in Coetzee's series of subtle experiments with point of view and voice, *Summertime*, a book that by various external signs declares itself to be a sequel to *Boyhood* and *Youth* and thus a memoir, perhaps fictionalized to some extent. The subtitle is once again "Scenes from Provincial Life," and the blurb of the first Australian edition claims that "it completes the majestic trilogy of fictionalised memoir begun with *Boyhood* and *Youth*." And indeed, the book begins with a section of "Notebooks 1972–75," short extracts, none longer than four pages, in the familiar dry, depressive third-person voice, recounting incidents in the existence of a bachelor living with his father in a suburb of Cape Town. At the end of each extract, there is a brief italicized memorandum to himself, notes which would seem intended to show that this is a work in progress rather than a polished work ready for publication. Despite these metafictional signals, however, the reader familiar with Coetzee's work might find herself surprised by the absence of the kind of new approach one has come to expect from him. One might even feel a little dispirited at the prospect of 250 pages of this rather drab narrative stretching ahead. However, this disappointment—surely deliberately aroused—does not last beyond the first twenty pages, as we are plunged into a quite new scenario. Although one has assumed that the notebook entries are John Coetzee's, it is not until the beginning of the next section, titled "Julia," that this is confirmed. In alternating passages of italics and plain text signaling questions and answers, we are led to understand that a former acquaintance of Coetzee's is being interviewed by a biographer, eventually identified as Mr. Vincent. They are talking of him in the past tense, but it still comes as a shock when Julia says, "Since he is dead, it can make no difference to him…" (*S* 37). This book has now departed as far from autobiography as did *Diary of a Bad Year*. From now on, we are unable to trust the factual basis of anything in *Summertime*, and doubt is cast by association on *Boyhood* and *Youth* as well.

Julia's narrative, studded with Mr. Vincent's probings and promptings and occasionally his silence (noted in brackets, as if this is a transcript of an audio recording), is in the first person, quite naturalistic. Julia does not just tell her story but draws attention to her subjectivity and the inexactness of her narrative: "as far as the dialogue is concerned, I am making it up as I go along. Which I presume is permitted, since we are talking about a writer" (*S* 32). She is also adamant (like Lucy in *Disgrace*) that she is not a minor character in this narrative, that the story she is telling is hers, not Coetzee's:

> The only story involving John that I can tell, or the only one I am prepared to tell, is this one, namely the story of my life and his part in it, which is quite different, quite another matter, from the story of his life and my part in it. … You commit a grave error if you think to yourself that the difference between the two stories, the story you wanted to hear and the story you are getting, will be nothing more than a matter of perspective—that…by dint of a quick flip, a quick manipulation of perspective, followed by some clever editing, you can transform it into a story about John and one of the women who passed through his life. (*S* 43–44)

Susan Barton is avenged: the whole interview with Julia is included, in her own words, occupying one-quarter of the book's pages.

The next interviewee is Margot Jonker. This is Vincent's second meeting with her, and he explains how he is planning to proceed:

> After I got back to England I transcribed the tapes of our conversations. … Then I did something fairly radical. I cut out my prompts and questions and fixed up the prose to read as an uninterrupted narrative spoken in your voice.
>
> What I would like to do today, if you are agreeable, is to read through the new text with you. (*S* 87)

He proceeds to do so, interrupted from time to time by her protests about unsuitable word choices and passages she wants omitted. In one instance, she refuses to let him include something about her sister Carol:

> *I won't let you write that. You can't write that about Carol.*
> It's what you told me.

Yes, but you can't write down every word I say and broadcast it to the world. I never agreed to that. Carol will never speak to me again.

All right, I'll cut it out or tone it down, I promise. (*S* 100–101)

A passage like this seems to pull both ways. The book is based on the premise that what is presented is the raw material of a biography, not the finished product, and it lacks the polish of a finished narrative. So far, it seems to be masquerading as fact, with realistic dialogue between two people with different agendas. However, the very fact that these conversations are included and the objectionable passages are not left out proves otherwise: if this had any basis in fact, it could not have been published. It, more than anything else in the book, proves that this is a work of fiction.

One of Margot's complaints is the choice of the third-person pronoun for her narrative. Vincent reads a sentence:

And of the four, she alone, she suspects, looks back to the old days with nostalgia.

I don't understand. Why do you call me she?

Of the four, Margot alone, she—Margot—suspects, looks back with nostalgia…You can hear how clumsy it is. It just doesn't work that way. The *she* I use is like *I* but is not *I*. (*S* 89)

Strangely, he doesn't point out that this use of the third-person pronoun echoes Coetzee's own practice in *Boyhood* and *Youth*. She lets it pass, but a couple of pages later, she stops him again.

When I spoke to you, I was under the impression that you were simply going to transcribe our interview and leave it at that. I had no idea you were going to rewrite it completely.

That's not entirely fair. I have not rewritten it, I have simply recast it as narrative. Changing the form should have no effect on the content. If you feel I am taking liberties with the content itself, that is another question. Am I taking too many liberties?

I don't know. Something sounds wrong, but I can't put my finger on it. (*S* 91)

Little is divulged about Vincent's background and qualifications as Coetzee's biographer, but clearly he is not a literary scholar if he believes that form has no effect on content.

Margot is John's cousin, the young girl who appears, as Agnes, in *Boyhood*, to whom he could talk about "everything, everything he did, everything he knew, everything he hoped for" (*B* 94) during their holidays at the family farm, Voëlfontein. They had childish plans of marrying, and she retains a "lingering soft spot" for him (*S* 89). She defends him to her sister, who is inclined to be unfriendly and overcritical, but when his ineptitude forces her to spend a night alone with him in his truck, she finds herself revising her opinion of him: "[S]he feels bitter because she had hoped for much from John, and he has failed her. … Because of the Coetzee men he was the one blessed with the best chance and he did not make use of it" (*S* 115). A later conversation is also included, where Margot suggests John "write a best-seller. Make lots of money":

> It is only a joke, but he chooses to take it seriously. "I wouldn't know how to write a best-seller," he says. "I don't know enough about people and their fantasy lives. Anyway, I wasn't destined for that fate…The fate of being a rich and successful writer." (*S* 149)

He has told her that he is not writing—or at least not writing poetry. She doesn't believe him but doesn't know that he is writing fiction and never refers to his later career as a writer. Vincent rounds off her part of the book shortly after this conversation, so we are not able to find out whether Margot's faith in John is restored by the publication of his books.

The next interview is with a Brazilian woman whose daughter was taught English by Coetzee at her high school in Cape Town. Adriana Nascimento had been concerned about his credentials as an English teacher: she thought from his name that he must be an Afrikaner. She meets him and begins to suspect him of evil designs on her daughter, suspicions he inflames by expounding his Platonic theory of learning: "The true student burns to know. In the teacher she recognizes, or apprehends, the one who has come closer than herself to the truth" (*S* 163). However, despite her misgivings, she soon finds herself the object of his ardor, or "perhaps what he really wanted was both of us…mother and daughter" (*S* 192). She finds him "just an irritation, an embarrassment…to me he really was a fool" (*S* 193). Vincent attempts to improve Adriana's opinion of Coetzee by suggesting that he based the character of Susan Barton on her. She is not convinced but promises to read the book: "I am interested to see what this man of wood made of me" (*S* 201).

The interview with Julia had also been mainly concerned with the sexual relationship between John and herself, in reasonably unflattering terms, but Adriana all but accuses him of pedophilia and stalking; this whole section is very uncomfortable reading for an admirer of Coetzee.

The next interview is with Martin, a colleague from the University of Cape Town. It begins with another extract from a notebook which Vincent reads out loud, introducing it by saying, *"As you will hear, he follows the same convention as in* Boyhood *and* Youth, *where the subject is called 'he' rather than 'I'"* (*S* 205). Martin's assessment is that

> John was a perfectly adequate academic…but not a notable teacher…He told me once that he had missed his calling, that he should have been a librarian. I can see the sense in that. (*S* 212)

But as the interview proceeds and Vincent asks about "special friendships" with his students, Martin starts wondering about the direction this biography is taking: "It seems to me strange to be doing the biography of a writer while ignoring his writing" (*S* 218), a sentiment which most readers will surely endorse. Nevertheless, the next interview, although it is also with a university colleague, is with a French woman with whom Coetzee had an affair. She is more inclined to be discreet about their *liaison* than Julia, but she, like Martin, is less than enthusiastic about his academic ability—"not spectacular but competent. Always well prepared" (*S* 223)—and dismisses his books as "too cool, too neat. … Too lacking in passion" (*S* 242).

The book ends with more fragments from the notebooks, mainly concerning Coetzee's father and the problems of caring for him in his declining years. The final thought of the book is that he is faced with the prospect of devoting himself to nursing his father, or else "he must announce to his father: *I cannot face the prospect of ministering to you day and night. I am going to abandon you. Goodbye.* One or the other: there is no third way" (*S* 266).

If regarded as a piece of self-revelation, *Summertime* is excoriating. The only person who seems to have any enthusiasm for Coetzee as man or writer is the biographer Vincent, who betrays his naivety in several ways: Martin, for example, cautions him that "it would be very, very naïve to conclude that because the theme [of the older man and the younger woman] was present in his writing it had to be present in his life" (*S* 215). *Summertime* is full of little messages like this, but their provenance is so compromised by the layers of perspectives that their truth value can never be established. And yet, this book is so self-critical that it seems to be obeying some profound confessional urge that begs the reader to contradict the harsh judgments it makes. The fact that so much of it is distanced from his own voice seems to be saying on the one hand that this is an objective view, but then on the other hand that this *is* a work by Coetzee. However much he impersonates other characters, his is the guiding consciousness behind the book. And the final impression, the stubborn fact that the reader keeps bumping up against, is that this is an extraordinarily solipsistic book, despite the elaborate distancing devices. What game is Coetzee playing here? What point is he making? What should we make of Martin's remark that "a strain of secretiveness …seemed to be engrained in him, part of his character" (*S* 212)? Is this work a convoluted and rather perverse means of guarding his secrets? A memoir may never have an uncomplicated relationship with the facts, but in this case, there is so little genuine self-revelation that one might be forgiven for suspecting that *Summertime* is intended as a reproof to biographers and those who enjoy reading their wares.

ENDNOTE

1. See, for example, Henson; Lawlan 131–157; Scanlan 463–477.

CHAPTER 4

THE COMIC ARTS

"One does not, of course, 'like' Coetzee. ... Revolted by the body, uncontaminated by humor, renouncing irony without finding commitment, Coetzee's fictions do not offer themselves to our 'liking'," says Regina Janes (103). But humor and comedy are arguably unavoidable in the novel. Iris Murdoch, a novelist who was also a philosopher and thought deeply about the nature of her form, said,

> I think the novel is a comic form. I think tragedy is a highly specialized and separate form. Doubtless it's the highest of all art forms, but it depends on certain limitations which a novel can't have. The novel is always comic. (25)

This is not to say that Coetzee's novels (or any others) will necessarily provoke laughter, of course, but humor is often present in the texture of the prose, and the outlines of his novels always hold a comic shape. Coetzee could not write about Michael K's teaspoon or David Lurie's dead dogs if he had no sense of the ridiculous.

I realize that I am pitting myself against some formidable critical opinion in making this claim. Having read claims like that of Janes quoted earlier, I was encouraged to see that James Wood had included a chapter on Coetzee in his book *The Irresponsible Self: On Laughter and the Novel*, in which he discusses

> the comedy of what I want to call "irresponsibility" or unreliability, [which] although it has roots in Shakespearean comedy, it seems to me the wonderful creation of the late nineteenth- and early twentieth-century novel. This comedy, or tragicomedy, of the modern novel replaces the knowable with the unknowable, transparency with unreliability, and this is surely in direct proportion to the growth of characters' fictive inner lives. (10)

This, in Wood's skillful hands, promised to be a fruitful and unusual way of looking at Coetzee's fiction. However, the chapter "Coetzee's *Disgrace*: A Few Skeptical Thoughts" seems to be included principally with the intention of showing him to be an anomaly. Coetzee's novels, according to Wood, "avoid the warm flavours of the comic-ironic for the bitter concentrates of the allegorical-ironic. (And is one not always a little suspicious of a writer without any comic impulse at all?)" (*Irresponsible* 246–247). And then, Ian Buruma, reviewing *Youth*, wrote,

> With one little tweak, these travails would be hilarious, the stuff of dark comedy. Perhaps...Coetzee is in fact making fun of himself. But I don't think so. ... The Afrikaner blood runs thickly in his English prose. And that blood contains a tendency toward dogmatism. (53)

Coetzee might be answering such critics when in *Summertime* he has several of the interviewees mention John's comic sensibility. Julia, for example, says:

> He ran his life according to principles, whereas I was a pragmatist. Pragmatism always beats principles: that is just the way things are. ... Principles are the stuff of comedy. Comedy is what you

get when principles bump into reality. I know he had a reputation for being dour, but John Coetzee was actually quite funny. (*S* 63)

John's colleague Martin does not regard their position as white South Africans as tragic, "and I am sure he did not either":

> If anything, it was comic. His ancestors in their way, and my ancestors in theirs, had toiled away, generation after generation, to clear a patch of wild Africa for their descendants, and what was the fruit of all their labours? Doubt in the hearts of those descendants about title to the land; an uneasy sense that it belonged not to them but, inalienably, to its original owners. (*S* 210)

One could link the dark, brutal comedy of *Dusklands* to this kind of attitude. Both Eugene Dawn and Jacobus Coetzee throw themselves uncomprehendingly against history and bounce back, not unscathed but not destroyed either. Their actions are ludicrous as well as horrific. It is also perhaps a feature of a certain genre of black comedy that, as Martin might be suggesting, the comic suffering of the self-absorbed perpetrators is foregrounded while the tragic suffering of the victims of their actions is belittled and discounted. The intended effect of this is, of course, ironic: the reader is tacitly encouraged to reverse the emphasis.

My first encounter with Coetzee's writing was at an evening session of the ACLALS (Association for Commonwealth Literature and Language Studies) Conference in Canberra in 2001, when he read extracts from a work in progress that turned out, as he kindly but monosyllabically advised me afterwards, to be *Youth*. It convinced me straight away, despite his quiet and deadpan delivery, that Coetzee was a comic writer. How could Professor Buruma miss the comedy in John's meditations on Ganapathy's failure to turn up for lunch?

> Is there something about the whole business that he has failed to understand, something Indian? Does Ganapathy belong to a caste to which it is taboo to eat at the table of a Westerner? If so, what is he doing with a plate of cod and chips in the Manor House canteen? Should the invitation to lunch have been made more

formally and confirmed in writing? By not arriving, was Ganapathy graciously saving him the embarrassment of finding a guest
at his front door whom he had invited on an impulse but did
not really want? Did he somehow give the impression, when he
invited Ganapathy, that it was not a real, substantial invitation he
was extending, merely a gesture towards an invitation, and that
true politeness on Ganapathy's part would consist in acknowledging the gesture without putting his host to the trouble of providing
a repast? Does the notional meal (cold meats and boiled frozen
peas with butter) that they would have eaten together have the
same value, in the transaction between himself and Ganapathy,
as cold meats and boiled frozen peas actually offered and consumed? Is everything between himself and Ganapathy as before,
or better than before, or worse? (*Y* 148)

Perhaps it needs to be read aloud for full comic effect, but even read
silently, the humorous elements are plain: the repetition in each sentence
of the name Ganapathy, the perfectly constructed sentences, carefully
avoiding solecisms such as ending in a preposition or using a nomina-
tive pronoun in place of an accusative, the relentless build-up of angst
and insecurity to a climax of worry about the future of his friendship,
interspersed with absurd details—"cod and chips in the Manor House
canteen," "cold meats and boiled frozen peas with butter."

Buruma talks of dogma, but the dogma in *Youth* belongs to the character, whose foolish beliefs are implicitly mocked by the narrator. Young
John's dogma is concerned with art and how it is forged:

Suffering, madness, sex: three ways of calling down the sacred
fire upon oneself. He has visited the lower reaches of suffering,
he has been in touch with madness; what does he know of sex?
Sex and creativity go together, everyone says so, and he does
not doubt it. Because they are creators, artists possess the secret
of love. The fire that burns in the artist is visible to women, by
means of an instinctive faculty. (*Y* 66)

The comic element in John's adherence to this dogma is, of course, that
while we can see that it is inadequate and misleading, he sees *himself* as

inadequate to its exacting principles, and this is a source of excruciating and very funny anxiety:

> If no woman has yet detected, behind his woodenness, his clenched grimness, any flicker of the sacred fire…does it mean that he is not a real artist, or does it mean that he has not suffered enough yet, not spent enough time in a purgatory that includes by prescription bouts of passionless sex? (*Y* 67)

It is inconceivable that a writer who could imagine "a purgatory that includes by prescription bouts of passionless sex" is "a writer without any comic impulse at all" (J. Wood, *Irresponsible* 246–247). Dominic Head, at least, agrees that "*Youth*…is often funny, most especially when [John's] doubts and scruples give way to open self-mockery" (*Cambridge* 14).

Youth is, I admit, an unusually funny book for Coetzee—possibly his funniest. I wrote in chapter 2 that *Disgrace* contains little comedy. Shortly after writing that, I reread the novel and discovered two jokes on the first two pages. In this case, the jokes are not directed at the protagonist; they are his own. He visits Soraya, a prostitute, weekly. He says, "Technically he is old enough to be her father; but then, technically, one can be a father at twelve" (*D* 1). Not hilarious, but a dig in the ribs nonetheless. On page 2, he announces that "his temperament is not going to change, he is too old for that. His temperament is fixed, set. The skull, followed by the temperament: the two hardest parts of the body" (*D* 2). These two pleasantries—perhaps *jokes* is, after all, too strong a word—help build up the picture of the complacent, ironic, and rather smug being that is David Lurie, a picture that anyone who understands the way stories work knows will soon crack and will be shattered by the end of the novel. Later in the novel, such localized humor as there is—and I don't claim that it is pervasive—reflects a more desperate state of mind. "If Lucy has any sense," Lurie thinks, "she will quit before a fate befalls her worse than a fate worse than death" (*D* 134). Despite his anxiety and desperation, Lurie has not lost his penchant for ironic wordplay: the "fate worse than death," that coy melodramatic euphemism for loss of virginity, becomes grimly comic when applied to Lucy's rape, especially in the context of this sentence, which contradicts itself by imagining an even worse fate, one which he does not want to put into words even in his thoughts, and deflects by conceiving of it in this flippant way. He and Lucy watch television in the evenings, "the news and then, if they can bear it, the entertainment" (*D* 141). After apartheid, South African television has not improved much, it seems, though its torments are presumably of a different nature from those that caused Elizabeth Curren to scream at Vercueil to switch it off in *Age of Iron*, "[b]ecause I am afraid of going to hell and having to listen to *Die stem* for all eternity" (*AI* 181).

David Lurie's sense of irony is strong: Lucy calls it "that terrible irony of yours. … For years you used it against me when I was a child, to mortify me" (*D* 200). This is one of the many difficult things he has to hear from his daughter: he has to learn to vacate the position of superiority that sarcasm implies, to stop being witty. Instead of sharpening his wit on Bev Shaw's ministrations to dying animals, he learns from her "to concentrate all his attention on the animal they are killing, giving it what he no longer has difficulty in calling by its proper name: love" (*D* 219). In *Summertime*, John notes the limits of irony: "To the barbarians, as Zbigniew Herbert has pointed out, irony is simply like salt: you crunch it between your teeth and enjoy a momentary savour: when the savour is gone, the brute facts are still there" (*S* 16). The ironic stance is easy and clever and may encourage some fellow-feeling among like-thinking people, but it can be personally destructive while achieving nothing against the real enemies, the "barbarians" running the state under apartheid. This may explain why, after *Dusklands*, dramatic irony has a diminishing place in Coetzee's work.

In the early novels, Coetzee's humor can be savage. Both Eugene Dawn and Jacobus Coetzee are appallingly comic at times. The very first sentence of *Dusklands* is an invitation to a comic flight: "My name is Eugene Dawn. I cannot help that. Here goes" (*DL* 1). Over the cliff, down the slope, for a vertiginous trip into madness. Dawn, in his dissociative state, laughs at the most monstrous things:

> I find something ridiculous about a severed head. One's heartstrings may be tugged by photographs of weeping women come

to claim the bodies of their slain; a handcart bearing a coffin or even a man-size plastic bag may have its elemental dignity; but can one say the same of a mother with her son's head in a sack, carrying it off like a small purchase from the supermarket? I giggle. (*D* 16)

We do not laugh with him (if we are sane); we wince in horror. Later, in the motel room with his young son Martin, we see Dawn attempting to be a writer—and, incidentally, a father:

> I have *Herzog* and *Voss*, two reputable books, at my elbow, and I spend many analytic hours puzzling out the tricks which their authors perform to give to their monologues (they are after all no better than I, sitting day after day in solitary rooms secreting words as the spider secretes its web...) the air of a real world through the looking-glass. A lexicon of common nouns seems to be a prerequisite. Perhaps I was not born to be a writer.
>
> Meanwhile Martin plays quietly on the floor beside me. ... When he has had enough of the bear family Martin will re-read the adventures of Spider Man or play behind the wheel of my car, building up rich emulative fantasies until it is time for lunch. ...
>
> I am going to have to come to terms with the laundry. (*D* 36)

The comic effect of the last sentence is clear: the absurd juxtaposition of the quotidian with Martin's "rich emulative fantasies" and Dawn's more absurd fantasies of being able to emulate Saul Bellow and Patrick White. But the comedy in "The Vietnam Project" is not just an occasional joke: it is woven through the texture of the story, inseparable from Dawn's highly unreliable narration—in his self-absorption and disregard of his victims, for example.

The equally appalling narrator in "The Narrative of Jacobus Coetzee" is not so easy to mock, but he has moments of insecurity in his megalomania, as expressed in one of Coetzee's earliest strings of comic questions:

> [The Hottentots'] failure to enter more deeply into me had disappointed me. They had violated my privacy, all my privacies,

> from the privacy of my property to the privacy of my body. They
> had introduced poison into me. Yet could I be sure I had been
> poisoned? Had I not perhaps been sickening for a long time, or
> simply been unused to Hottentot fare? If they had poisoned me,
> had they poisoned me with a penetrating, a telling, an instructional
> poison, on the principle of to every man his own meat, or, unfamil-
> iar with poisons, had they underdosed me? But how could savages
> be unfamiliar with treachery and poisons? But were they true sav-
> ages, these Namaqua Hottentots? Why had they nursed me? Why
> had they let me go? Why had they not killed me? Why had their
> torments been so lacking in system and even enthusiasm? Was I
> to understand the desultory attentions paid me as a token of con-
> tempt? Was I personally unexciting to them? Would some other
> victim have aroused them to a pitch of true savagery? (*D* 97)

And so it continues, until his chilling last question, "Was there nothing to
be done to make them take me more seriously?" (*D* 98). We might laugh
at this point, but later we realize that this train of thought has lead inexo-
rably, through wounded pride and outraged prejudice, to the destruction
of the Namaqua village and the slaughter of its inhabitants.

A gentler comedy is to be found in *Life & Times of Michael K.* Michael
has a way of finding moments of joy in the midst of an impossibly difficult existence. His mother is in a hospital, dying, in a strange town
where they know nobody. There is no chair by the hospital bed, nowhere
to sit, so he goes outside:

> A man in the hospital yard fell into conversation with him. "You
> here for stitches?" he enquired. K shook his head. The man
> looked critically at his face. Then he told a long story of a tractor
> that had toppled over on him, crushing his leg and breaking his
> hip, and of the pins the doctors had inserted in his bones, silver
> pins that would never rust. He walked with a curiously angled
> aluminium stick. "You don't know where I could get something
> to eat," asked K. "I haven't eaten since yesterday." "Man," said
> the man, "why don't you go and get us both a pie," and passed K
> a one-rand coin. K went to the bakery and brought back two hot
> chicken pies. He sat beside his friend on the bench and ate. The
> pie was so delicious that tears came to his eyes. The man told

him of his sister's uncontrollable fits of shaking. K listened to the
birds in the trees and tried to remember when he had known such
happiness. (*MK* 29–30)

This passage is funny and touching at the same time: the kindness of
the man, who asks nothing for his gift but a passive listener; Michael's
capacity to be moved to tears and unexampled happiness by a chicken
pie and birdsong, while not being troubled by the man's medical horror
stories or the fact that his mother is about to die and that he is homeless.
The comedy certainly does not draw the reader to identify with Michael:
we are not laughing with him in complicity as we are with, say, David
Lurie in the early stages of *Disgrace* or Elizabeth Curren in *Age of Iron*,
when she complains about her body:

> [T]hese legs, these clumsy, ugly stilts: why should I have to carry
> them with me everywhere? Why should I take them to bed with
> me night after night and pack them in under the sheets, and pack
> the arms in too, higher up near the face, and lie there sleepless
> amid the clutter? (*AI* 13)

With Michael, we are being shown a new way of being, one perhaps to be
smiled rather than laughed at. James Wood proposes that the "comedy of
forgiveness…can be distinguished…from the comedy of correction. The
latter is a way of laughing at; the former a way of laughing with" (*Irresponsible* 6). We do not laugh with Michael, but neither do we quite laugh
at him. Laughing at him would mean that we disapprove of him and think
he should change. Coetzee succeeds in creating an unusual type of fictional
character in Michael, one that does not develop. This novel, he says,

> didn't turn out to be a book about *becoming* (which might have
> required that K have the ability to adapt, more of what we usually
> call intelligence) but a book about *being*, which merely entailed
> that K go on being himself, despite everything. (Morphet 455)

In the end, Michael is rather like a cartoon character who is indestructible,
whatever he has to endure. The medical officer is the one who changes,

and it seems to me we laugh both *at* and *with* him as he imagines himself shouting existential questions at a receding Michael, desperate for a response.

Humor in Coetzee's fiction is rarely communal: it often contributes in some way to a character's isolation. The characters' own jokes, if they make them, are usually strictly personal, not to be shared with others: in *Disgrace*, Lucy tells David to give his "terrible irony" a rest, and in *Slow Man*, Marijana fails to laugh at Paul Rayment's jokes:

> He cannot remember her ever responding to his humour. Is he too frivolous for her taste? Does she find him too light, too lightweight, too much of a joker? Or is she simply not sure enough of her English to bandy words? (*SM* 173)

On the other hand, Marijana's own humor does not make him laugh: "Nothing subtle about it. He ought to adjust, if he aspires one day to be her mystical bridegroom" (*SM* 184). He keeps his jokes about her husband and his imagined "elemental Balkan rages that give birth to clan feuds and epic poems" to himself, realizing that "he makes jokes about Jokic because he envies him" (*SM* 51).

In fact, Coetzee's characters usually find other people's jokes unamusing. The play in which Melanie acts, *Sunset at the Globe Salon*, is viewed coolly by David Lurie, professor of English:

> On stage a hairdresser, flamboyantly gay, attends to two clients, one black, one white. Patter passes among the three of them: jokes, insults. Catharsis seems to be the presiding principle: all the coarse old prejudices brought into the light of day and washed away in gales of laughter. (*D* 23)

It is laughter in which he is clearly not joining. He sees the play again towards the end of the book.

> The holidaymakers among whom he is seated, ruddy-faced, comfortable in their heavy flesh, are enjoying the play. They have taken to Melanie-Gloria; they titter at the risqué jokes, laugh uproariously when the characters trade slurs and insults.

> Though they are his countrymen, he could not feel more alien among them, more of an impostor. Yet when they laugh at Melanie's lines he cannot resist a flush of pride. (*D* 191)

Humor rarely creates a sense of fellow-feeling or integration, even when that is the intention. Elizabeth Costello approaches the guardian at the gate:

> "If you keep rejecting my statements I'll have to take up residence with you in your lodge," she says. "I can't afford hotel rates."
>
> It is a joke, she just means to shake up this rather dour fellow.
>
> "For long-term petitioners," he replies, "there is a dormitory. With kitchen and ablution facilities. All needs have been foreseen."
>
> "Kitchen or soup kitchen?" she asks. He does not react. Evidently they are not used to being joked with in this place. (*EC* 197)

There are several occasions in *Summertime* when the interviewee laughs, apparently along with the interviewer, at John. This happens particularly in the interview with Adriana: she has described him as "an ordinary little man...tepid," who "fell in love rather easily," and then they laugh (*S* 196–197). They laugh at Vincent's description of him as "dogged": "being like a dog—is that admirable, in English?" (*S* 197). Sophie's laughter is possibly more of a nervous reaction, though when Vincent asks her for "*more personal stories from your time together*," she replies, "Stories of his kindness towards animals—animals and women? No, those stories I will be saving for my own memoirs," and laughter follows (*S* 235–236), suggesting, perhaps, that the very idea that such stories exist may be ludicrous. In any case, the impression in both cases is of James Wood's comedy of correction rather than of forgiveness, laughing at John slightly maliciously, not affectionately with him. This certainly seems true of Adriana's mocking laughter. Sophie, however, later adds,

> Looking back, I now see our relationship as comical in its essence. Comico-sentimental. Based on a comic premise. Yet with a further element that I must not minimize, namely, that he helped me

escape from a bad marriage, for which I remain grateful to this day. (*S* 241)

Early in *Boyhood*, John shares a joke with his father. It brings them together briefly, but the humor is an expression of pure male aggression against his mother:

> Every time his father sees the heavy black bicycle leaning against the wall he makes jokes about it. In his jokes the citizens of Worcester interrupt their business to stand and gape as the woman on the bicycle labours past. *Trap! Trap!* they call out, mocking her: Push! There is nothing funny about the jokes, though he and his father always laugh together afterwards. As for his mother, she never has any repartee, she is not gifted in that way. "Laugh if you like," she says. (*B* 3–4)

Despite this early training in the masculine art of bullying through humor, John, like his mother, has failed to develop the art of repartee by his early twenties:

> The crisis is bringing out the best in Londoners, they say, who confront adversity with quiet strength and a ready quip.
>   As for him, he may dress like a Londoner, tramp to work like a Londoner, suffer the cold like a Londoner, but he has no ready quips. (*Y* 102)

His girlfriend Caroline asks "[w]hy does he not come out of himself, have some fun? 'Some of us are not built for fun,' he replies. She takes it as one of his little jokes, does not try to understand" (*Y* 77). She knows him very imperfectly if she interprets his dourness as "little jokes": the reader realizes by now that his sense of humor is as yet pitifully under-developed. However, Julia, one of John's former lovers interviewed in *Summertime*, remembers his friendship after their affair in the 1970s had ended: "When I felt low I could always rely on him to joke with me and lift my spirits" (*S* 81), though his gaiety on the occasion of the publica-tion of *Dusklands* was "a side of him" that she seldom saw (*S* 55). But they do share jokes: in the early stages of their acquaintance, it is clearly

John's dry wit which attracts her rather than any physical attributes; she recalls a joke about Sumerian mathematics and a playfully ironic reference to the attractions of Muzak at the supermarket where they first meet. She saw him as "a figure of comedy. Dour comedy. Which, in an obscure way, he knew, even accepted" (*S* 63).

One characteristic of many of Coetzee's protagonists is a self-conscious sense of their own ridiculousness. Pathological in Jacobus Coetzee's rage at being belittled by the Namaqua, this embarrassment becomes something to be overcome and learned from in David Lurie's case and is a source of much of the comedy in *Slow Man*. Paul Rayment refuses to sue Wayne Blight, the driver of the car that knocked him off his bicycle, because it provides "too many openings for comedy" (*SM* 15). Marijana's son makes his old bicycle into a recumbent:

> Of course he will never put it to use. … Do they know that?…
>
> For a moment he allows himself to imagine he is rolling down Magill Road, the pennant fluttering brightly overhead to remind the world to have mercy on him. A perambulator, that is what it is most like: a perambulator with a grizzled old baby in it, out for a ride. How the bystanders will smile! Smile and laugh and whistle: *Good on you, grandpa!*
>
> But perhaps, in a larger perspective, that is exactly what the Jokics mean to teach him: that he should give up his solemn airs and become what he rightly is, a figure of fun. (*SM* 256)

A few pages later, Elizabeth Costello makes much the same point about Drago's theft and digital alteration of his historic photograph: "Of course it is just a joke…Directed against you. Whom else? The man who doesn't laugh. The man who can't take a joke" (*SM* 259). But, even though Costello tells him that "losing a leg is comic. Losing any part of the body that sticks out is comic. Otherwise we would not have so many jokes on the subject" (*SM* 99), Paul is not able to relax gracefully into the role of the figure of fun, which makes him, of course, yet more of a figure of fun. J. C. in *Diary of a Bad Year* is equally self-conscious, though not as prickly and more able to see other points of view sympathetically, especially after his interaction with Anya, and much of the comedy of the novel is softened and defused almost into sentimentality.

In Margot's narrative in *Summertime*, the Coetzee family's sense of humor is seen as a strategy to avoid difficult truths:

> As soon as their ease is threatened, the Coetzees rush in with jokes. A family drawn up in a tight little *laager* to keep the world and its woes at bay. But how long will the jokes go on doing their magic? (*S* 126)

John himself writes in his notebook, "[A]ll they want is to get along with everyone and have a bit of a laugh in the process" (*S* 247). But, unlike the rest of the family, "[i]n the laughing department he is the last companion his father needs. In laughing he comes bottom of the class" (*S* 248). He is harder on himself than Julia, who remembers their conversations as "fun: I enjoyed them; I missed them afterwards" (*S* 62). There is a marked contrast between his view of his own "clenched grimness" (*Y* 67) and the comic view his books often put forward. "A gloomy fellow: that must be how the world sees him. A gloomy fellow; a wet blanket; a stick in the mud" (*S* 248), he says in *Summertime*. The self-pity expressed here is comic, and the implied author is holding the character of John up for ridicule.

Samuel Beckett's comic characters have none of this self-consciousness. It is hard to imagine Watt or Murphy taking the trouble to wonder what people thought of them. Yet, it is Beckett who finally gives John an idea of what sort of writer he might be, in *Youth*:

> *Watt* is quite unlike Beckett's plays. There is no clash, no conflict, just the flow of a voice telling a story, a flow continually checked by doubts and scruples, its pace fitted exactly to the pace of his own mind. *Watt* is also funny, so funny that he rolls about laughing. When he comes to the end he starts again at the beginning.
>
> Why did people not tell him Beckett wrote novels? How could he have imagined he wanted to write in the manner of [Ford Madox] Ford when Beckett was around all the time? In Ford

> there has always been an element of the stuffed shirt that he has
> disliked but has been hesitant to acknowledge, something to do
> with the value Ford placed on knowing where in the West End
> to buy the best motoring gloves or how to tell a Médoc from a
> Beaune; whereas Beckett is classless, or outside class, as he him-
> self would prefer to be. (*Y* 155)

Coetzee has not quite freed himself from that Fordian constraint, or, at
least, his characters have not. It may not be a matter of class, as it would
be in an Englishman, but his characters are always conscious of a certain superiority, with the exception, of course, of Michael K. The Magistrate's humiliation in *Waiting for the Barbarians* is largely contingent on
his previous position of privilege and power in the town. Paul Rayment
has second thoughts about Marijana when he sees her at home, "wearing
blue plastic sandals…and purple toenails. … Their aesthetics are worlds
apart" (*SM* 244). Aesthetics are a strong indicator of class: Paul is not
just implying here that his tastes are *different* from Marijana's; he thinks
his tastes are *better* than hers, and this makes him realize how incompatible they are. In *Doubling the Point*, he talks about his youthful attraction to Ford:

> The kind of aestheticism Ford stood for struck a chord in me:
> good prose was a matter of cutting away, of paring down…; novel-
> writing was a craft as well as a vocation; and so forth. But I now
> suspect that there was more to the attraction than that. Ford gives
> the impression of writing from inside the English governing class,
> but in fact he wrote as an outsider, and as a somewhat yearning
> outsider at that . … Ford's social aspirations drove him to become
> in many ways *plus anglais que les anglaises.* He cultivated a kind
> of gruff stoicism, which he thought of as Tory…and embodied in
> his hero Christopher Tietjens. I now suspect that what attracted
> me to Ford was as much the ethics of Tietjens as the aesthetics of
> *le mot juste.* (*DP* 20)

The spareness and the "gruff stoicism" can still be traced in many of Coetzee's novels, but many of the comic passages, the long strings of rhetorical questions, for example, owe more to Beckett than Ford. The delight

Beckett taught him to take in the absurd and the ridiculous has, I am sure, contributed more to Coetzee's popularity than many critics realize. He told Attwell in *Doubling the Point* that

> Beckett's prose, up to and including *The Unnamable*, has given me a sensuous delight that hasn't dimmed over the years. The critical work I did on Beckett originated in that sensuous response, and was a grasping after ways in which to talk about it: to talk about delight. (*DP* 20)

Perhaps the grimness of much of Coetzee's prose sets his occasional comic passages into a starker contrast, making the reader laugh with surprise. And perhaps delight is not the most obvious word to use to describe the effect of Coetzee's writing. However, surprise and delight certainly play their part in "what it is that grips and compels us as we read, producing an experience, disturbing and pleasurable at the same time, of new possibilities at the very limits of our habitual thoughts and feelings," as Attridge puts it ("Against Allegory" 73). The comedy in Coetzee's books is often veiled and only becomes apparent on a rereading. In the same way that I failed to notice the jokes in *Disgrace* at first, my initial impression of *Summertime* was of an unrelievedly grim, self-lacerating work. On a second reading, more relaxed about what was to come, I could see moments of humor and even began to wonder whether the whole book were not in fact intended as an extended joke directed against all the earnest and humorless readings his novels have attracted.

The novel is a comic form: it does not lend itself to tragedy. It may be grim, violent, and appalling, but life goes on, and the novel seems unable to ignore this. *"No other way than death,"* says J. C. in *Diary of a Bad Year*, "is a marker and perhaps even a definition of the tragic" (*DBY* 21). Novels often begin with a death, but they concern themselves mainly with survivors, and survivors are comic figures. Coetzee's novels tend to look most comic when viewed in outline. The Beckettian figure of endurance ("I can't go on, I'll go on" [Beckett 179]) prefigures David Lurie with his dead dogs, Paul Rayment with his crutches, and the Magistrate picking up the pieces after his ordeal in *Waiting for the Barbarians*:

> Above all it is food that I crave, and more intensely with every passing week. I want to be fat again. There is a hunger upon me day and night. I wake with my stomach yawning, I cannot wait to be on my rounds, loitering at the barracks gate to sniff the bland watery aroma of oatmeal and wait for the burnt scrapings; cajoling children to throw me down mulberries from the trees; stretching over a garden fence to steal a peach or two; passing from door to door, a man down on his luck, the victim of an infatuation, but cured now, ready with a smile to take what is offered. …
> And how I can flatter, how I can woo! (*WB* 129)

Elizabeth Costello at the gate is not permitted to pass through before the novel ends. She receives the ultimate insult, for one who thinks of herself as remarkable, from the guard: "We see people like you all the time" (*EC* 225). The skeletal Michael K thinks he can stay alive by drawing water from a disused well with a teaspoon, and he may be right. Magda has to reconcile herself to the dismal fact

> that I may have long to wait before it is time to creep into my mausoleum and pull the door shut behind me, always assuming that I can find a pair of hinges in the loft, and drift into a sleep in which there are finally no voices teasing or berating me. (*HC* 138)

Elizabeth Curren is borne away in the embrace of death, it is true, but what a grotesque embrace it is, embodied in a skinny, dry, old homeless man. Regina Janes asks, "How is one to 'like' a writer who turns over our lives, our politics, our traditions, our literature, who fingers our western culture, our common humanity, even our alterity, and says—is that all? Really no more than this?" (103). Even though at times the comedy heightens the horror, perhaps if there were no comedy in Coetzee, we would find him unbearable. Critics who have found him lacking in humor might look again and see that the comic impulse, while not making Coetzee a comic novelist in the usual sense, is actually an integral part of his whole approach to fiction.

CHAPTER 5

LANGUAGE AND LANGUAGES

> Ideas are certainly important—who would deny that?—but the
> fact is, the ideas that operate in novels and poems, once they are
> unpicked from their context and laid out on the laboratory table,
> usually turn out to be uncomplicated, even banal. Whereas a style,
> an attitude to the world, as it soaks in, becomes part of the person-
> ality, part of the self, ultimately indistinguishable from the self.
> (Coetzee, "Homage" 7)

In the last chapter, I made what might appear to be a contentious claim
about comedy in Coetzee's work. In this chapter, I am on firmer ground:
as Steven G. Kellman says, "The relations between words and thought,
the boundaries between one language and another, and the limits of language have been central to Coetzee's concerns as both a novelist and a
scholar" (161). It is hardly controversial to claim that much of Coetzee's
appeal is related to his highly developed sense of the nature and possibilities of language. His interest and expertise in linguistics, explicit in
his literary criticism, are implicit everywhere in his fiction. As he told
Jean Sévry,

> Much of my academic training was in Linguistics. And in many
> ways I am more interested in the linguistic than the literary side
> of my academic profession. I think there is evidence of an interest
> in problems of language throughout my novels. I don't see any
> disruption between my professional interest in language and my
> activities as a writer. (Sévry 1)

In *Doubling the Point*, Coetzee admits that he "quite laboriously
search[es] out the right word":

> I do believe in spareness—more spareness than [Ford Madox]
> Ford practiced. Spare prose and a spare, thrifty world: it's an
> unattractive part of my makeup that has exasperated people who
> have had to share their lives with me. (*DP* 20)

Exasperating perhaps on a personal level, but spareness is one of the
salient characteristics of Coetzee's prose that most critics applaud. However, James Wood, in his essay "Coetzee's *Disgrace*: A Few Skeptical
Thoughts," writes,

> Coetzee is always praised for his dignified bleakness, for the
> "tautness" or carefulness or grim efficiency of his prose, which
> is certainly good enough to embarrass the superfluous acreage of
> many supposedly richer stylists. But there is a point beyond which
> pressurized shorthand is no longer an enrichment but an impov-
> erishment, and an unnatural containment. It is the point at which
> ellipsis becomes a formalism, a kind of aestheticism, in which
> fiction is no longer presenting complexity but is in fact converting
> complexity into its own too-certain language. (249)

In particular, he complains that Coetzee's description of Melanie's boyfriend in *Disgrace* is "only the beginning of a description": "no-one is
ever adequately described as simply 'tall and wiry…a thin goatee and
an ear-ring…black leather jacket'" (250). But, it could be argued that
this kind of sketch is precisely what is required for this minor character
in this context. It is not necessary to present complexity in every aspect
of a novel. The "free indirect style" in which the novel is narrated means
that this description is not an "objective" view of the character from

a disinterested narrator but Lurie's own impression, encompassing not only the boyfriend's physical appearance but some hint of his insolence and the threat he represents, conveyed by the tautness of the language.

Another aspect of this impressionistic style is the present tense that Coetzee uses in *Disgrace*. As John Mullan says, this is an uncommon choice in combination with the third person:

> Why does Coetzee use it? Because it gives to the narrative voice a numbed, helpless quality. Lurie is intelligent and self-analytical, yet somehow powerless to shape his life. His emotions bleached by disillusion, he succumbs to sexual impulse. The normal past tense of narrative…would have implied some vantage point beyond the events of the story. Usually we look back in the company of a narrator from the other side of an ending. The pattern of a story has been decided, even if we do not yet grasp it. The present tense, however, makes everything provisional. It edges us closer to the situation of the character while refusing us any actual identification with him. (72)

The threat to Lurie's comfortable life is thus implicit not only in the complacent beginnings of the novel but also in the narrative style. John Douthwaite points out that in the opening sentence of *Disgrace*, "[t]he smugness and self-satisfaction Lurie expresses, th[r]ough infringing the politeness principle by uttering self-praise, thereby flaunting anti-social behaviour…underscore his individualistic attitude."[1] However,

> his values and attitudes are being challenged while they are being conveyed. … The novel sets out with a theme, a point of view, a challenge to that point of view, and with an ironic comment on a supposedly cultured and highly articulate person who in actual fact does not know what is happening to him and around him, or does not want to know. (Douthwaite, "Coetzee's *Disgrace*" 47)

As Rita Barnard writes,

> [A] crisis of definitions, relationships, and responsibilities lies at the heart of *Disgrace*. This crisis is investigated on the level of

> fundamental linguistic structures—both grammatical and lexical.
> The novel's free indirect narration conveys a curious sense that word
> choices are imperfect, still in the process of being made. (206)

In fact, in every one of Coetzee's narrative works from *The Master of
Petersburg* to *Slow Man*—that is, nearly half of his oeuvre—he writes in the
present tense with a third-person narrator. Are the powerlessness and help-
lessness that Mullan identifies in David Lurie characteristic of all the main
characters of these six books: the tormented Fyodor Dostoevsky in *The Master of Petersburg*; John Coetzee, anxious in *Boyhood* and miserable in *Youth*;
the benighted David Lurie in *Disgrace*; Elizabeth Costello in her eponymous
book (but not in *Slow Man*); and the doleful Paul Rayment in *Slow Man*?
Many of these characters appear to be acting on conscious choices, but in
fact, they are often stalled into inaction for some reason or driven by external
events or internal impulses which seem beyond their control.

The present tense has been Coetzee's choice in almost all of his
books. The main exceptions are "The Narrative of Jacobus Coetzee" and
Michael K's narrative in *Life & Times of Michael K*. Parts of *Age of Iron*
are in the past—when Elizabeth Curren is relating past events to her
daughter—but the narrative present of the novel is in the present tense.
And in *Foe*, the tense at first similarly depends on whether Susan Barton is relating past events in her narrative or writing letters to Mr. Foe
about her activities in the present. However, part 3, narrated by Susan in
the first person, is in the past tense with no narrative framing—without
the quotation marks of the first two parts—and part 4, the indeterminate
first-person epilogue, is in the present tense. Usually, then, Coetzee's
past tense belongs to a first-person narrator (Elizabeth Curren, Jacobus
Coetzee, or Susan Barton). The two exceptions are Michael K's sections
of *Life & Times of Michael K* and part 3 of *Foe*.

What does this mean? The present tense seems more fluid, less fixed.
James Harrison sees the first-person present tense in *Waiting for the Barbarians* as allowing

> the reader to participate in the magistrate's self-discovery…Coe-
> tzee enables the reader to remain abreast of a first-person narrator

who is grappling with the events of the novel and, however imperfectly, assessing and reassessing his own response to them in retrospect. (81)

On the other hand, *Life & Times of Michael K* is, as Coetzee says, a novel about being rather than becoming (Morphet 455), so the past tense suits him better than Coetzee's more usual present tense, in which the characters develop in ways they cannot foresee in reaction to events they do not expect. Formally, we are seeing Michael's story from a distance in time as well as viewpoint. In part 3 of *Foe*, the use of the more conventional past tense might be linked with the questioning of such narrative conventions: Susan wonders why, "in the same room as yourself at last, where I need surely not relate to you my every action…I continue to describe and explain" (*F* 133). At the end of part 3, Foe and Susan discuss the characters of this narrative. Foe asks Susan,

> "Has the time not come to tell me the truth about your own child, the daughter lost in Bahia? Did you truly give birth to her? Is she substantial or is she a story too?"
> "I will answer, but not before you have told me: the girl you send, the girl who calls herself by my name—is she substantial?"
> "You touch her; you embrace her; you kiss her. Would you dare to say she is not substantial?"
> "No, she is substantial, as my daughter is substantial and I am substantial; and you too are substantial, no less and no more than any of us. We are all alive, we are all substantial, we are all in the same world."
> "You have omitted Friday." (*F* 152)

To remedy this omission, the epilogue that follows takes us to "the home of Friday," which is "not a place of words," and uses the present tense to mark it off from this fictional "place of words" where a possibly bogus substantiality has been achieved and captured in the past tense (*F* 157).

Despite the generally acknowledged spareness in Coetzee's prose, there is a certain tendency to flights of the imagination, always, of course, on the part of the character. James Wood says,

> Coetzee's chaste, exact, ashen prose may look like the very
> embers of restraint, but it is drawn, again and again, to passion-
> ate extremity. ... Coetzee seems compelled to test his celebrated
> restraint against subjects and ideas whose extremity challenges
> novelistic representation. ("Squall Lines" 140)

Sophie Mayroux points out that

> Coetzee's sentences are meant to achieve a precise effect, to build
> stone by stone the microcosm of each novel, in the same way as a
> data-processing programme proceeds towards a given goal from
> one instruction to another. Such an application of scientific rigor
> to literature is akin to a puritanical ethos. (9)

Nevertheless, "I would not like people who have not read Coetzee to
be misled into thinking that his style is austere or bleak" (9). I have discussed his long strings of rhetorical questions already, the way they present a character's preoccupations and anxieties, often in a comic vein.
He also often uses an extended metaphor or string of similes to convey
a character's feelings in an almost exuberant way that can seem to contradict those feelings. After the attack in *Disgrace*, Lurie experiences "a
taste of what it will be like to be an old man":

> Slumped on a plastic chair amid the stench of chicken feathers
> and rotting apples, he feels his interest in the world draining from
> him drop by drop. It may take weeks, it may take months before
> he is bled dry, but he is bleeding. When that is finished, he will be
> like a fly-casing in a spiderweb, brittle to the touch, lighter than
> rice-chaff, ready to float away. ...
>   Just an after-effect, he tells himself, an after-effect of the inva-
> sion. In a while the organism will repair itself, and I, the ghost
> within it, will be my old self again. But the truth, he knows, is
> otherwise. His pleasure in living has been snuffed out. Like a leaf
> on a stream, like a puffball on a breeze, he has begun to float
> towards his end. (*D* 107)

Such a pile-up of figurative images might seem unexpected in a writer
known for his "spareness." Firstly, there is the metaphor of his interest

in the world draining away like blood; then he is "like a fly-casing" which is itself "lighter than rice-chaff." Not content with floating like the fly-casing/rice-chaff, he again likens himself to "a leaf on a stream" and a "puffball on a breeze." All these images of lightness counteract his despair at the same time as they describe it, make this ending seem less painful, perhaps unconsciously providing himself with consolation for the heavy, grey mood which has descended on him. Coetzee's third person is rarely detached from his character's point of view—as Douthwaite says, "The third-person narrative could be written as first-person narration without having to make many or radical changes to the text. Thus what is superficially heterodiegetic narration is, in deep structure, homodiegetic" ("Coetzee's *Disgrace*" 55). The voice, and thus the imagery, belongs to David Lurie, not to an invisible third-person narrator.

Paul Rayment has a similar moment in *Slow Man*, although his self-pity is more comical than David Lurie's. Paul feels "on the brink of one of his bad spells again, one of the fits of lugubrious self-pity that turn into black gloom":

> Why…can he not resist these plunges into darkness?
> The answer is that he is running down. Never is he going to be his old self again. Never is he going to have his old resilience. …
> A memory comes back to him of the cover of a book he used to own, a popular edition of Plato. It showed a chariot drawn by two steeds, a black steed with flashing eyes and distended nostrils representing the baser appetites, and a white steed of calmer mien representing the less easily identifiable nobler passions. Standing in the chariot, gripping the reins, was a young man with a half-bared torso and a Grecian nose and a fillet around his brow, representing presumably the self, that which calls itself *I*. Well, in his book, the book of him, the book of his life, if that ever comes to be written, the picture will be more humdrum than in Plato. Himself, the one he calls Paul Rayment, will be seated on a wagon hitched to a mob of nags and drays that huff and puff, some barely pulling their weight. After sixty years of waking up every blessed morning, munching their ration of oats, pissing and shitting, then being harnessed for the day's haul, Paul Rayment's team will have had enough. (*SM* 53)

These extended flights—Rayment's horse-drawn fantasy continues for another couple of sentences—are most likely to occur in those scenes where a character is alone, ruminating on his situation, whereas the business of narrating events and describing settings and other characters is couched in sparer prose. This kind of self-patterning with word-pictures goes back as far as "The Vietnam Project":

> I was brought up on comic-books. … Enthralled once to monsters bound into the boots, belts, masks, and costumes of their heroic individualism, I am now become Herakles roasting in his poisoned shirt. For the American monster-hero there is relief: every sixteen pages the earthly paradise returns and its masked savior can revert to pale-faced citizen. Whereas Herakles, it would seem, burns forever. There are significances in these stories that pour out of me, but I am tired. (*DL* 32)

From the Heart of the Country is practically all made up of this kind of self-imagination, with occasional interruptions of more prosaic narrative. As Magda says, "I create myself in the words that create me" (*HC* 8). The internal wrangling of his characters, with gods and ghosts and ideas, is where much of the energy of Coetzee's work is focused, rather than the plots and settings. This may be another reason for his persistent use of the present tense, which best suits his characters' subjective, existential, questioning angst. His characters even argue with the nature of the language they are forced to use. In a postscript to *Elizabeth Costello*, Elizabeth Chandos rails against metaphor: "It is like a contagion, saying one thing always for another (*like a contagion*, I say)" (*EC* 228). And J. C. complains in *Diary of a Bad Year* about common politico-economic metaphors:

> The figure of economic activity as a race or contest is somewhat vague in its particulars, but it would appear that, as a race, it has no finishing line and therefore no natural end. The runner's sole goal is to get to the front and stay there. The question of why life must be likened to a race, or of why the national economies must race against one another rather than going for a comradely jog together, for the sake of the health, is not raised. (*DBY* 64)

Despite the jocular tone, he has a serious point. "Dud metaphor[s]" like the race and the jungle are used by governments to urge people to work harder and make more money:

> Behind this rebuke to the otiose life (*otium*: leisure time which may or may not be used for self-improvement) and justification of unceasing business lie assumptions that no longer need to be articulated, so self-evidently true do they seem: that each person on earth must belong to one nation or another and operate within one or other national economy; that these national economies are in competition with one another. (*DBY* 63–64)

Typically for a Coetzee character, he questions these assumptions by analyzing the false metaphors they are based on, but then, in turn, allows his questioning to be undercut by Anya's point of view. Later, in the essay "On English Usage," he points out that

> [m]ost scientists can't write for toffee, yet in their professional life who practises exact thinking better than they? Might the uncomfortable truth...not be that ordinary people use language as exactly as they feel to be required by the circumstances...and... that lapses of concord or bizarreries of syntax...make no practical difference? (*DBY* 120–121)

Perhaps everyday interpersonal communication can take place without "linguistic correctness," but unthinking use of clichéd metaphors can result in faulty reasoning by anyone, not only politicians but also scientists unless they are on their guard, because the language can become infected with figurative language that becomes invisible once overused—like a contagion, as Elizabeth Chandos writes. In *Summertime*, the notebooks towards the end of the book contain an idea for a story. A writer finds his diary entries becoming more and more gloomy. He cannot write poetry or prose. He becomes suicidal.

> All of his intercourse with the world seems to take place through a membrane. Because the membrane is there, fertilization will not take place. It is an interesting metaphor, full of

> potential, but it does not take him anywhere that he can see. (*S* 261)

That concludes the fragment: a metaphoric dead-end, giving him no help with his problem. Even mathematics, "which we believe or hope to be a key to the structure of the universe, may equally well be a private language—private to human beings with human brains—in which we doodle on the walls of our cave" (*DBY* 79).

Many of Coetzee's characters wield language self-consciously, especially the narrators and third-person focalizers. Many are writers or scholars or linguists who think about the etymology of the words they use and are conscious of the vocabulary of other languages. Coetzee is bilingual by heritage, growing up in an extended family in which both English and Afrikaans were spoken. Kellman believes that

> translingualism sensitised Coetzee to the powers and deficiencies of any system—linguistic or political. To adopt another language is to cultivate empathy for alternative modes of apprehension. A rejection of self-sufficient, totalising regimes, such negative capability is the most profound form of insurrection. (171)

Asked about the meaning of "being sent to an Afrikaner school, consigned, as you put it [in *Boyhood*], to an Afrikaans' life," Coetzee responded that it meant

> first of all, being consigned to the Afrikaans half of the school I was attending but, more frighteningly, it would have meant being drawn into the bosom of the Dutch Reformed Church and the National Party, of the whole cultural crusade of the times to erect a distinct and unique white Afrikaner national being. And for a rather timid child this was an alarming prospect. (Wachtel 38)

This was apparently not just an individual attitude. In *Summertime*, Sophie Denoël recalls discussing John's family with him:

> Somehow or other that wave of nationalist enthusiasm passed John's family by. ... First they were disturbed by the whipped-up

hostility to everything English, by the mystique of *blut und Boden*;
then later they recoiled from the politics that the nationalists took
over from the radical right in Europe. (*S* 239–240)

Nevertheless, although his feelings about Afrikaners are fearful and hostile, he recounts in *Boyhood* that,

> to his surprise, he finds himself unwilling to yield up the Afri-
> kaans language to them. ...
>   When he speaks Afrikaans all the complications of life seem
> suddenly to fall away. Afrikaans is like a ghostly envelope
> that accompanies him everywhere, that he is free to slip into,
> become at once another person, simpler, gayer, lighter in his
> tread. (*B* 125)

He likes "the happy, slapdash mixture of English and Afrikaans" his
extended family speaks. "He likes this funny, dancing language, with
its particles that slip here and there in the sentence" (*B* 81), though he
despises

> the circumlocutions of Afrikaans. Afrikaners are afraid to say *you*
> to anyone older than themselves. He mocks his father's speech:
> "*Mammie moet 'n kombers oor Mammie se knieë trek anders
> word Mammie koud*"—Mommy must put a blanket over Mom-
> my's knees, otherwise Mommy will get cold. He is relieved he
> is not Afrikaans and is saved from having to talk like that, like a
> whipped slave. (*B* 49)

In *Youth*, he finds it embarrassing when a visiting South African girl
speaks Afrikaans to him in the London of the 1960s. "Speaking Afrikaans in this country, he wants to tell her, is like speaking Nazi, if there
were such a language" (*Y* 127). Afrikaans is part of his national identity
that he wants to be rid of: "South Africa is like an albatross around his
neck. He wants it removed, he does not care how, so that he can begin to
breathe" (*Y* 101). On his return to South Africa in the 1970s, according
to his cousin Margot in *Summertime*, John's Afrikaans is "halting." He
makes mistakes, but "they have spoken Afrikaans together since they

were children: she is not about to humiliate him by offering to switch,"
even though her English is better than his Afrikaans (*S* 93).

It seems hardly surprising, then, that Coetzee has chosen to write in
English. He has explained his choice in an interview:

> What I like about English and what I certainly don't find in Afri-
> kaans, what does not exist in Afrikaans, is a historical layer in the
> language that enables you to work with historical contrasts and
> oppositions in prose—prose is my medium. Secondly, there is a
> genetic diversity about the language, which after all is not only a
> Germanic language with very heavy romance overlays, but is also
> a language which is very receptive to imported neologisms so that
> macaronic effects are possible—you can work with contrasts in
> the etymological basis of words. Macaronic effects are available
> to a writer in English that are simply absent certainly in, shall we
> say, official Afrikaans, and are only to a very limited extent avail-
> able if you use a colloquial Afrikaans very heavily impregnated
> with importation from English. From that point of view Afrikaans
> as a linguistic medium is to me—frankly dull. (Sévry 2)

Nevertheless, *From the Heart of the Country* was published in a South
African edition in which much of the dialogue is in Afrikaans and the
narrative in English.[2] Brian McCaskill notes,

> It becomes even more obvious here than in the English-language
> edition that one of the central subjects of this novel is the struggle
> against subjection by language. Far from being an escapist retreat
> from the protopolitics of cultural production and the interventions
> of history or economy, Coetzee's text goes to the very heart of
> such matters: their inescapably linguistic formulation. (464)

In each of the other South African novels—*Life & Times of Michael K,
Age of Iron,* and *Disgrace*—English is the language of the main character. Michael K's narrative is monolingual, though the medical officer
records some dialogue in Afrikaans. Elizabeth Curren encounters Afrikaans on occasion, in the mouths of officials like the soldier, a "boy
with pimples playing this self-important, murderous game," whom she

meets on the night of Bheki's death (*AI* 105). David Lurie seems to be exposed to very little Afrikaans, only hearing its echoes in the "glaringly *Kaaps*" accent Melanie assumes for her role in *Sunset at the Globe Salon* (*D* 23). For both these academics schooled in the culture of Europe, other languages hold more significance. Nevertheless, there is a telling anecdote in *Summertime*. Sophie, his French colleague, recounts how a French journalist enraged John by calling Afrikaans "an obscure dialect" (*S* 237). She goes on to say, "He knew Afrikaans well, I would say, though in much the same fashion as he knew French, that is, better on the page than spoken" (*S* 238). However, he felt a degree of identification with Afrikaans quite different to his attitude to French: Sophie believes that he was a "marked Francophile" who would have liked a particular kind of "French mistress" who would conform to his fantasies (*S* 241). Afrikaans, on the other hand, was part of his personal identity, and he resented the French journalist's "insult to [its] dignity" (*S* 237).

In *Youth*, we learn that John has tried to learn French "but his efforts have got him nowhere. He has no feel for French. … The language resists him, excludes him; he cannot find a way in" (*Y* 75). This is not because he has no facility for languages:

> He knows Latin…He picks up Spanish without difficulty. … The language for which he has a real feeling, however, is German… With the ghost of Afrikaans still in his ears, he is at home in the syntax. In fact, he takes pleasure in the length of German sentences, in the complex pileup of verbs at the end. There are times, reading German, when he forgets he is in a foreign language. … [B]ut he knows no one else who reads German poetry, just as he knows no one who speaks French. …
>
> There remains Holland. At least he has an insider's knowledge of Dutch, at least he has that advantage. Among all the circles in London, is there a circle of Dutch poets too? If there is, will his acquaintance with the language give him an entrée to it?
>
> Dutch poetry has always struck him as rather boring, but the name Simon Vinkenoog keeps cropping up in poetry magazines. … He reads everything there is by Vinkenoog in the British Museum, and is not encouraged. … If Vinkenoog is all that

> Holland can offer, then his worst suspicion is confirmed: that of
> all nations the Dutch are the dullest, the most antipoetic. So much
> for his Netherlandic heritage. He might as well be monolingual.
> (*Y* 75–77)

Latin, Spanish, German, Dutch, Afrikaans, and some knowledge of
French: from another narrator this could sound boastful, but John manages, comically, to convert his multilingualism into yet another reason for
misery and self-deprecation. In *Disgrace*, likewise, David Lurie reflects
that his knowledge of European languages is of no use in communicating
with the men who have locked him in Lucy's lavatory: "He speaks Italian, he speaks French, but Italian and French will not save him here in
darkest Africa" (*D* 95). This represents one more stage in his increasing
consciousness of how inadequately his education has prepared him for
life in modern South Africa. His narrative is full of "macaronic effects,"
words and phrases drawn not only from French and Italian but Latin and,
frequently, German. He calls the killing of the dogs carried out at the
animal welfare clinic "*Lösung* (German always to hand with an appro-
priately blank abstraction)" (*D* 142), an abstraction haunted by the Nazis'
use of *endlösung* or "final solution," allowing the tacit suggestion of a
comparison between the "mercy killings" of the dogs and the Holocaust.

In *Age of Iron*, Elizabeth Curren sprinkles her narrative with words
from foreign languages—French, Italian, Afrikaans, and especially
Latin, which was her subject when she taught at the university. She has a
slightly pedantic way of narrating, as indeed do all Coetzee's narrators:
describing herself as she imagines Vercueil sees her, she talks of "the
skirt with whose hang there has always been something wrong" (*AI* 4).
She uses her knowledge of language equivocally to berate Vercueil:

> "What is the point of charity when it does not go from heart to
> heart?…*Charity*: from the Latin word for the heart. It is as hard to
> receive as to give." …
> A lie: charity, *caritas*, has nothing to do with the heart. But
> what does it matter if my sermons rest on false etymologies? He
> barely listens when I speak to him. (*AI* 22)

She has already felt the force of his powerful alinguistic communication:

> With a straight look, the first direct look he has given me, he spat a gob of spit, thick, yellow, streaked with brown from the coffee, onto the concrete beside my foot. …
>
> *The thing itself*, I thought, shaken: the thing itself brought out between us. Spat not upon me but before me, where I could see it, inspect it, think about it. His word, his kind of word, from his own mouth, warm at the instant when it left him. A word, undeniable, from a language before language. (*AI* 8)

However, Vercueil is not unreachable. After a while, she finds that "he was learning to talk to me. … After long silence it is such a pleasure: tears come to the eyes" (*AI* 76). It is a measure of their increasing companionship that towards the end of the book, he asks if she could teach him Latin. She often ponders words, their shapes and meanings:

> *Gratitude*: I write down the word and read it back. What does it mean? Before my eyes it grows dense, dark, mysterious. Then something happens. Slowly, like a pomegranate, my heart bursts with gratitude; like a fruit splitting open to reveal the seeds of love. *Gratitude, pomegranate*: sister words. (*AI* 56)

Sister words only in her mind, however, with its linguistically inclined imagination: they are not related etymologically. She seeks verbal similarities and connections with words that have arisen in her life. She has a dream about the battle of Borodino, brought on, she believes, by the Diconal tablets she has to take to help her sleep:

> Borodino, Diconal: I stare at the words. Are they anagrams? They look like anagrams. But for what, and in what language?…
>
> Borodino: an anagram for *Come back* in some language or other. Diconal: *I call.*
>
> Words vomited up from the belly of the whale, misshapen, mysterious. Daughter. (*AI* 138, 140)

These are not mere intellectual exercises. Elizabeth Curren endows words with deep emotional significance, even though, as Gilbert Yeoh claims, "the novel's sly implication is that her discourse may amount to nothing, while the marginalized voices of Vercueil, Thabane and John count for something" (122). After his accident, Paul Rayment, too, translates his pain, in his half-conscious state, into snatches of language:

> Something is coming to him. A letter at a time, *clack clack clack*, a message is being typed on a rose-pink screen that trembles like water each time he blinks and is therefore quite likely his own inner eyelid. E-R-T-Y, say the letters, then F-R-I-V-O-L, then a trembling, then E, then Q-W-E-R-T-Y, on and on.
> *Frivole.* Something like panic sweeps over him. (*SM* 3)

Frivole—French for *frivolous*. Paul Rayment ("rhyming with *vraiment*" [*SM* 192]) was born in France and still thinks in snatches of French language. He thinks of the stump of his amputated leg as "*le jambon. Le Jambon* keeps it at a nice, contemptuous distance" (*SM* 29). Behind his comprehension of English words like *care*, there is a shadow of a French phrase remembered from childhood:

> The more he stares at the words *take care of*, the more inscrutable they seem. He remembers a dog they had when he was a child in Lourdes, lying in its basket in the last stages of canine distemper, whimpering without cease, its muzzle hot and dry, its limbs jerking. "*Bon, je m'en occupe*," his father said at a certain point, and picked the dog up, basket and all, and walked out of the house. Five minutes later, from the woods, he heard the flat report of a shotgun, and that was that, he never saw the dog again. *Je m'en occupe*: I'll take charge of it; I'll take care of it; I'll do what has to be done. That kind of caring, with a shotgun, was certainly not what Marijana had in mind. Nevertheless, it lay englobed in the phrase, waiting to leak out. (*SM* 43–44)

Thinking about this French phrase, he produces the odd word *englobed*, a direct borrowing from the French *englober*, meaning to include or embody. Later, like Elizabeth Curren, he makes a consciously tenuous link between *care* and the heart: he imagines that Marijana may have

> accepted without afterthought what she was told by the accreditation board: that the profession into which she was being initiated was in the English-speaking world known as a caring profession; that her business would henceforth be taking care of people or caring for people; and that such caring should not be assumed to have anything to do with the heart, except of course in heart cases. (*SM* 165)

Imagining a letter he might write to Marijana, he thinks about this word: "*Care*: he can set the word down on paper but he would be too diffident to mouth it, make it his own speech. Too much an English word, an insider's word" (*SM* 165). Another word he finds foreign, as he tells Elizabeth Costello, is *home*:

> I have always found it a very English concept, home. ... Among the French, as you know, there is no *home*. Among the French to be at home is to be among ourselves, among our kind. I am not at home in France. Transparently not. I am not the *we* of anyone. (*SM* 192–193)

Immediately, he regrets his frankness and the way he has expressed himself: "*I am not the we of anyone*: how does she manage to extort such words from him?" (*SM* 193). In another of their argumentative conversations, Costello wonders,

> Does it all come down to the English language, to your not being confident enough to act in a language that is not your own?... You speak English like a foreigner. ... The more I listen the more convinced I am that the key to your character lies in your speech. You speak like a book. (*SM* 230–231)

This idea, of language being basic to the human condition and embodied, is pervasive in Coetzee's work. Interestingly, Coetzee's French translator,

Sophie Mayroux, identifies as one of the keys to his unique style his non-English background:

> Coetzee writes very slowly and carefully, going several times over his text, working and re-working on it from one version to the next. The result is so elaborate that I sometimes got the feeling of an artificial language, a forgery, as if the work was already a—very good—translation. ... When trying to describe Coetzee's masterful handling of language and its literary uses, the term which comes to me and strikes me as central is *distance*.
>
> This distance is that of a man, born and bred in a country of many different—and antagonistic—languages, who has chosen not to write in his mother-tongue, rejecting Afrikaans in favour of English. (8)

This overstates the case. Coetzee's mother's language literally *was* English: though her parents were not English, his mother was brought up speaking English at home, and "her English is faultless" (*B* 106). In a 1993 article, Coetzee wrote:

> Though I have spoken English since childhood, I was not brought up in a culture that anyone would recognize as English. English in South Africa is what one might call a deeply entrenched foreign language; and there is a sense in which I have always approached English as a foreigner would, with a foreigner's sense of the distance between himself and it. This has not implied any linguistic insecurity: since childhood I have felt confident that I write English better than most natives. ("Homage" 7)

So his consciousness of bilinguality contributes to the distance or alienation Mayroux detects: although "he commands [the English language] with ease," he knows he will never "be accepted as truly English" (*B* 129), and being accepted as Afrikaner is not something he desires, so one of the defining characteristics of his childhood was an easy command of two languages, neither of which he could feel belonged to him.

In *Diary of a Bad Year*, Anya has a more playful multilingual style than J. C. He uses Latin words and occasionally talks about words and their derivations, but it is Anya, who presumably knows Spanish from her Philippine background, who makes bilingual puns in her narrative:

> At first I was supposed to be his segretaria, his secret aria, his scary fairy, in fact not even that, just his typist, his tipitista, his clackadackia. ...
> Segretaria. It sounds like a cocktail from Haiti. (*DBY* 25–26)

There is no sense in her narrative of any of the discomfort that Paul Rayment feels about English, though J. C. notices that she makes comical errors in her typing: "According to Daniel Defoe, I read, the true-born Englishman hates 'papers and papery.' Brezhnev's generals sit 'somewhere in the urinals'" (*DBY* 23–24). She blames it on spell-check. "Spellcheck has no mind of its own, I say. If you are prepared to hand it over to spellcheck to run your life, you might as well throw dice. We are not talking about life, she says. We are talking about typing" (*DBY* 24–25). On the other hand, she is confident enough to slight J. C.'s command of the language:

> Your English is very good, considering, but we don't say talk radio, that doesn't make sense, we say talkback radio.
> Considering? he said. Considering what?
> Considering it isn't your mother tongue. (*DBY* 44–45)

This is one of the topics that leaks back into his essays from the narrative sections. In "On the Mother Tongue," he ponders,

> Perhaps—is this possible?—I have no mother tongue. ... In a way that is, precisely, inarticulate, inarticulable, English does not feel to me like a resting place, a home. It just happens to be a language over whose resources I have achieved some mastery. (*DBY* 156–157)

A few pages earlier, J. C. had referred to "my novel *Waiting for the Barbarians*" (*DBY* 139). Identification between J. M. Coetzee the author and J. C. the character sometimes seems very close in these essays—closer than the facts of the parallel narrative would suggest—and it may be permissible to infer that they share such feelings.

Being at home in a language is as natural as singing. Elizabeth Costello tells Paul Rayment that a native speaker speaks "from the heart. Words well up within and he sings them, sings along with them" (*SM* 231). In the same vein, David Lurie finds the "first premise" of the Communications 101 course he has to teach "preposterous":

> "Human society has created language in order that we may communicate our thoughts, feelings and intentions to each other." His own opinion, which he does not air, is that the origins of speech lie in song, and the origins of song in the need to fill out with sound the overlarge and rather empty human soul. (*D* 3–4)

During his awkward encounter with Marianna, Paul Rayment asks her to sing: "Let me hear your voice. ... If you would sing, that would be best of all" (*SM* 103). The idea of singing often comes to Coetzee's characters at times when communication seems blocked. Fyodor Dostoevsky tries to explain to Anna Sergeyevna why he does not want to meet Nechaev and find out more about Pavel's death:

> To make her understand he would have to speak in a voice from under the waters, a boy's clear bell-voice pleading out of the deep dark. "Sing to me, dear father!" the voice would have to call, and she would have to hear. Somewhere within himself he would have to find not only that voice but the words, the true words. (*MP* 110–111)

This interest in singing must be linked to Coetzee's lack of sympathy with Beckett's later short fictions which are, "quite literally, disembodied. ...The late pieces speak in post-mortem voices. I am not there yet. I am still interested in how the voice moves the body, moves in the body" (*DP* 23).

There is a strong feeling in Coetzee that all music, not just singing, can be a form of speech, which excites a desire to communicate back to the composer. In his lecture "What Is a Classic?" he describes being transfixed, at the age of fifteen, by a recording of J. S. Bach's *Well-Tempered Clavier* overheard from a neighbor's house: "I was being spoken to by the music as music had never spoken to me before" (*SS* 8). It is interesting that he chooses an example from music, rather than literature, to illustrate this lecture—a response to T. S. Eliot's lecture of the same name, which concerned *The Aeneid.*

In *Summertime*, John recounts in his notebooks a struggle between his father and his teenage self over music, his father's love of Italian opera versus his own love of Bach. At sixteen, he destroyed his father's record of Renata Tebaldi, and "for that mean and petty deed of his he has for the past twenty years felt the bitterest remorse" (*S* 249). He buys another Tebaldi record and tries unsuccessfully to reach his father, desperate for his father to forgive him. But although his father seems unmoved, he begins to feel the power of this "sensual...decadent" music himself:

> What has been wrong with him all these years? Why has he not been listening to Verdi, to Puccini? Has he been deaf? Or is the truth worse than that: did he, even as a youth, hear and recognize perfectly well the call of Tebaldi, and then with tight-lipped primness ("I won't!") refuse to heed it? (*S* 251)

This might be one of the most amusing passages in *Summertime*: once again using the comic device of a string of rhetorical questions, he mocks not only his former intolerant attitude but also his present agony over what that attitude might betoken. Despite his conversion to Italian opera in the 1970s, it seems that Bach still speaks to Coetzee—he appears again in *Diary of a Bad Year*, in a heartfelt passage which it is difficult to discount as merely part of the fiction:

> The best proof we have that life is good, and therefore that there may perhaps be a God after all, who has our welfare at heart, is that to each of us, on the day we are born, comes the music of Johann Sebastian Bach. It comes as a gift, unearned, unmerited, for free.
>
> How I would like to speak just once to that man, dead now these many years! (*DBY* 173)

In one of his "grouchy" earlier essays, "On Music," J. C. complains about "the thudding, mechanical music favoured by the young":

> The bad drives out the good: what they call "classical" music is simply no longer cultural currency. Is there anything of interest to be said of the development, or must one just grouse about it under one's breath? (*DBY* 108)

Below this passage, in J. C.'s personal narrative, there appears the acknowledgment that opinions like these must appear "alien and antiquated…to a thoroughly modern Millie" (*DBY* 107–108), and this is one of the subjects he revisits. In the later passage, he seems to have realized that the music of J. S. Bach, like other classical music, is still freely available, despite the decline in its popularity that he detects. Perhaps he now feels that he can allow the young their enjoyment of their music without threat to his own feeling of "the history of music as a history of the feeling soul" (*DBY* 109).

Music as language appears occasionally in the earlier novels. Susan Barton, in *Foe*, somewhat optimistically thinks "that if there were any language accessible to Friday, it would be the language of music" (*F* 96). When her attempt to reach him through music fails, she believes that the reason is Friday's "disdain for intercourse with me" (*F* 98). The sexual echo is deliberate: she likens music-making to love-making. Elizabeth Curren senses Vercueil listening to her playing the piano and wonders whether the spirit of Bach has "made its way into the heart too of the man in the sagging trousers eavesdropping at the window? Have our two hearts, our organs of love, been tied for this brief while by a cord of sound?" (*AI* 24). More fortunate—or at least optimistic—in her communication via music-making than Susan Barton, Elizabeth later thinks, when she sees Vercueil again listening to Bach, "At this moment…I know how he feels as surely as if he and I were making love" (*AI* 30).

John, in *Summertime*, is singularly unsuccessful in his use of music as an aid to love. He brings a recording of Schubert's string quintet into the bedroom and tries to get Julia to "co-ordinate our activities to the music" (*S* 68). Julia is enraged:

> Franz Schubert becomes number one, the master of love: John becomes number two, the master's disciple and executant; and I become number three, the instrument on whom the sex-music is going to be played. That—it seems to me—tells you all you need to know about John Coetzee. The man who mistook his mistress for a violin. (*S* 83)

He also tries to woo the Brazilian woman, Adriana, with Schubert. He writes, in one of many letters sent during his unavailing pursuit of her, "that listening to Schubert had taught him one of the great secrets of love: how we can sublime love as chemists in the old days sublimed base substances" (*S* 175). Needless to say, Adriana is no more impressed by this than by his other attempts to attract her: "I was not interested in him. I just wanted him to keep his hands off Maria Regina" (*S* 176). Julia almost apologizes for telling the interviewer, Martin, about Schubert: "I never told anyone about that before you. Why not? Because I thought it would cast John in too ridiculous a light" (*S* 82). It is, indeed, one of the many parts of *Summertime* which makes John look ridiculous—or cold, or negligent, or incompetent, like his inability to dance, which Adriana, a dance teacher, believes makes John subhuman: "Dance is incarnation. ... Because the body knows. ... When the body feels the rhythm inside it, it does not need to think. That is how we are if we are human" (*S* 199). His rhetoric about feeling the music of Schubert within him has, according to these women (who are, of course, fictional constructs created by Coetzee), not helped him at all in his attempts to connect with another human being on an emotional or physical level, and the implication is that this is because it is purely intellectual. And his newly discovered response to Italian opera, which, according to the notebooks, happened shortly after he returned to South Africa (*S* 249), has clearly not helped either, though to him it seems a revolution involving both heart and soul.

David Lurie writes his chamber opera *Byron in Italy*, finding that

> he is in the opera neither as Teresa nor as Byron nor even as some blending of the two: he is held in the music itself, in the flat, tinny

slap of the banjo strings, the voice that strains to soar away from the ludicrous instrument but is continually reined back, like a fish on a line. (*D* 184)

Having expected to plunder other composers to set his words in a kind of musical pastiche, he has discovered Byron and Teresa "will demand a music of their own" (*D* 183). This is his answer to the question he has posed: "Can he find it in his heart to love this plain, ordinary woman? Can he love her enough to write a music for her? If he cannot, what is left for him?" (*D* 182). He tries, but the music he ends up writing is no masterpiece:

> The lyric impulse in him may not be dead, but after decades of starvation it can crawl forth from its cave only pinched, stunted, deformed. He has not the musical resources, the resources of energy, to raise *Byron in Italy* off the monotonous track on which it has been running since the start. ... His hopes must be more temperate: that somewhere from amidst the welter of sound there will dart up, like a bird, a single authentic note of immortal longing. (*D* 214)

In the end, he has to be content just to try without knowing whether he has succeeded, "[f]or he will not hear the note himself, when it comes, if it comes—he knows too much about art and the ways of art to expect that" (*D* 214). Any redemption must come through the endeavor rather than the achievement of negative capability.

Music can sometimes communicate where language cannot, but there are times when communication fails from a language's depletion. This is most often a political point, occurring in the South African novels. Jacobus Coetzee is "unsure whether my Hottentot, picked up at my nurse's knee and overburdened with imperative constructions, was compatible" with that of the Namaqua (*DL* 66). Magda exclaims,

> I cannot carry on with these idiot dialogues. The language that should pass between me and these people was subverted by my father and cannot be recovered. What passes between us now is a parody. I was born into a language of hierarchy, of distance and

perspective. It was my father-tongue. I do not say it is the language my heart wants to speak, I feel too much the pathos of its distances, but it is all we have. (*HC* 97)

She is talking not just of Afrikaans, but the particular variety of Afrikaans which is spoken between master and servant. John, in *Boyhood*, is embarrassed by the language of hierarchy on his relatives' farm. With the farm workers, "he has to speak tortuously constructed sentences to avoid calling them *jy* when they call him *kleinbaas*" (*B* 86). David Lurie, before he comes to dislike and mistrust Petrus,

> would not mind hearing Petrus's story one day. But preferably not reduced to English. More and more he is convinced that English is an unfit medium for the truth of South Africa. Stretches of English code whole sentences long have thickened, lost their articulations, their articulateness, their articulatedness. Like a dinosaur expiring and settling in the mud, the language has stiffened. Pressed into the mould of English, Petrus's story would come out arthritic, bygone. (*D* 117)

But Petrus himself is not unaware of the ironies of the language he shares with David Lurie and can use it for his own satirical purposes. "For digging," he says, "you just have to be a boy." Finding Petrus less interesting and likeable than he had at first, Lurie observes that "Petrus speaks the word with real amusement. Once he was a boy, now he is no longer. Now he can play at being one, as Marie Antoinette could play at being a milkmaid" (*D* 152).

Susan Barton, also, for all her goodwill towards Friday and her wish to communicate with him on equal terms finds that "there are times when benevolence deserts me and I use words only as the shortest way to subject him to my will" (*F* 6). Friday's muteness defeats her, demonstrating the inadequacy or perhaps irrelevance of her words in his world. It seems that Elizabeth Costello is making a related point when she explains that

> when we divert the current of feeling that flows between ourself and the animal into words, we abstract it for ever from the

> animal. … It falls within an entirely human economy in which the
> animal has no share. (*EC* 96)

Friday seems also to "have no share" in the economy of language in
which Foe and Susan make their transactions. The implication is not, of
course, that Friday is less than human, any more than Costello is saying that animals are lesser beings because they are outside the realm of
language. Muteness is also a characteristic of Michael K, in a sense. He
can speak, and he can understand language, but there are difficulties:
asked by a doctor, after his mother's death, whether he wanted to make
a phone call, he thinks, "This was evidently a code for something, he
did not know what" (*MK* 31). He has difficulties in understanding social
cues and communicating his feelings, though they may be strong. When
a family takes him in overnight on his journey and gives him food, muteness overcomes him:

> At the table the urge again came over him to speak. He gripped
> the edge of the table and sat stiffly upright. His heart was full,
> he wanted to utter his thanks, but finally the right words would
> not come. The children stared at him; a silence fell; their parents
> looked away. (*MK* 48)

The medical officer finds Michael's intermittent muteness exasperating and intriguing. He makes inaccurate assumptions from the little that
Michael tells him, such as his overinterpretation of Michael's relation of
his mother's cremation as "the vengeful mother with flaming hair who
comes to you in your dreams" (*MK* 149) and miscalling him "Michaels."
But Michael can afflict him with muteness as well:

> He shook his head from side to side, then without warning opened
> the great dark pools of his eyes on me. There was something more
> I had wanted to say, but I could not speak. It seemed foolish to
> argue with someone who looked at you as if from beyond the
> grave. (*MK* 148)

Muteness in Coetzee is rarely a sign of inadequacy. It is more usually a
recognition that another world of signs exists beyond language. Elizabeth

Curren, however, is "bereft of speech" on her encounter with the Afrikaans-speaking soldiers after seeing the bodies in the burnt-out hall (*AI* 105), and even when she begins to speak again is as unable to make them understand her as if they had no common language. When she talks to their officer, however, to her surprise, they can communicate:

> "Why don't you just put down your guns and go home, all of you?" I said. "Because surely nothing can be worse than what you are doing here. Worse for your souls, I mean."
> "No," he said. I had expected incomprehension, but no, he understood exactly what I meant. (*AI* 107)

It seems significant that the officer is speaking English rather than Afrikaans, which Curren usually associates with hostile, unresponsive officialdom. However, Vercueil, strangely, while he speaks English most of the time (or, at least, his dialogue is rendered in English), swears in Afrikaans when her servant Florence calls him "rubbish" and "good for nothing": "*Jou moer!*" he says, which translates as "your mother," that contemptuous age-old European insult (*AI* 47). This same expression shocks the Afrikaans-speaking Margot in *Summertime* when used against her in the waiting room in the Cape Town hospital where her mother has been brought from their country home: "*Jou moer!* —filthy talk. She must get her mother out as soon as she can" (*S* 150). It is a sign of "the loud, angry place this country has become" in the 1970s (*S* 151).

Though it isn't absolutely explicit, one can assume that Margot's narrative (as it is read out to her by Mr. Vincent in his recasting of it, and indeed the interview it is based on) is in English, as Vincent is English and knows little Afrikaans. The question of language is made more explicit in Adriana's interview, but only twenty pages in when she mentions the translator. Until then, we read without a thought for the language in which these two people—an English academic and a Brazilian dancer—are communicating. What we are reading, then, is (within the overarching fiction) a raw translation of the transcript of their interview. These reminders of the place of languages other than English in

Coetzee's world are slight but significant: he writes in English, but, as he tells Adriana, "there is nothing special about English. It is just one language among many" (*S* 161).

Elizabeth Costello, the writer from Melbourne, while she shares much with her creator, does not have Coetzee's polyglot sensibility, nor that with which he has endowed many of his characters. Though she knows enough German for a short conversation with the Russian singer on the Antarctic cruise, in Amsterdam she cannot understand what the Dutch child is saying in the washroom (*EC* 181). Her intellectual world is, as is more likely for an Australian, that of mainly English writers. Her best-known novel is based on characters from James Joyce's *Ulysses*; there is a discussion of Jonathan Swift—*A Modest Proposal* and *Gulliver's Travels*—in the seminar in the English Department of Appleton College. Her familiarity with Kafka, evident not only from the story "A Report to An Academy" that she discusses in her Pennsylvania lecture in lesson 1, but also from her sojourn at the gate in lesson 8, does not necessarily imply a deeper knowledge of German. Kafka's works are all readily available in translation, and she gives no clue to having read them in German.

Automatic reverence for the canon is, of course, not what one would expect from Coetzee, and indeed, we learn from *Boyhood* that Shakespeare did not particularly impress him in childhood:

> If his father likes Shakespeare then Shakespeare must be bad, he decides. Nevertheless, he begins to read Shakespeare, in the yellowing edition with the tattered edges that his father inherited... trying to discover why people say Shakespeare is great. (*B* 104)

However, he only reads *Titus Andronicus* and *Coriolanus* before he gets bored. Perhaps he becomes more engaged by the plays during his teens, because in *Youth*, he says "he is in the process of losing his taste for Shakespeare" as well as Gerald Manley Hopkins:

> Hopkins's lines are packed too tight with consonants, Shakespeare's too tight with metaphor. ... He does not see why verse has always to be rising to a declamatory pitch, why it cannot be

content to follow the flexions of the ordinary speaking voice—in fact, why it has to be so different from prose.

He has begun to prefer Pope to Shakespeare, and Swift to Pope. Despite the cruel precision of his phrasing, of which he approves, Pope strikes him as still too much at home among petticoats and periwigs, whereas Swift remains a wild man, a solitary.

He likes Chaucer, too. ... Chaucer keeps a nice ironic distance from his authorities. And, unlike Shakespeare, he does not get into a froth about things and start ranting. (*Y* 21)

This is a very telling summary of some of Coetzee's formative ideas about writing in his early twenties. The "cruel precision" of Pope, the solitary wildness of Swift, and the "ironic distance" of Chaucer seem all to have played their part in the evolution of his style, along with his fastidious rejection of Shakespearean "ranting." Shakespeare's plays, too, were used as an example of canonical works which might be left behind "to make room for the last speaker of Dyirbal" in his essay "Remembering Texas" (*DP* 52–53): perhaps it is significant that he did not choose another author. But Shakespeare does appear from time to time in the novels. Elizabeth Costello mentions him a couple of times in passing, rather dismissively, while her son, John, astronomer, pays him more attention:

Sleep, he thinks, *that knits up the ravelled sleeve of care*. What an extraordinary way of putting it! Not all the monkeys in the world picking away at typewriters all their lives would come up with those words in that arrangement. Out of the dark emerging, out of nowhere: first not there, then there, like a newborn child, heart working, brain working, all the processes of that intricate electro-chemical labyrinth working. A miracle. (*EC* 27)

Elizabeth Curren, too, comes to Shakespeare in her sleep. Her cancer preoccupies her: during her waking hours, her

true attention is all inward, upon the thing, the word, the word for the thing inching through my body. ...

Most of the time I am careful to hold the letters of the word apart like the jaws of a trap. When I read I read warily, jumping over lines or even whole paragraphs when from the corner of an eye I catch the shadow of the word waiting in ambush.

But in the dark, in bed, alone, the temptation to look at it grows too strong. ... It is a relief to stop resisting. ... I allow the wind to take me.

It takes me, night after night, to *The Merchant of Venice.* ..."Do I not bleed like you?" come the words of the Jew with the long beard and skullcap dancing in rage and anguish on the stage. (*AI* 39–40)

J. C., in *Diary of a Bad Year*, writes of Kurosawa's "Shakespearean clarity and comprehensiveness" (*DBY* 6) and quotes *The Tempest*: "You taught me language and my profit on it is I know how to curse" (*DBY* 30). And Anya finishes her narrative on a Shakespearean note, imagining herself at his deathbed: "Good night, Señor C, I will whisper in his ear: sweet dreams, and flights of angels, and all the rest" (*DBY* 178). The quotation from *Hamlet* may be a sign that she has learned something from him, as he has learned from her, since there are few other references to high culture in her narrative, despite her lively propensity for multilingual wordplay. J. C. notes that she "went to international schools all over the place (Washington, Cairo, Grenoble). What benefit she derived from that international schooling is not clear. She speaks French with an accent the French probably find charming but has not heard of Voltaire" (*DBY* 60).

In *Disgrace*, the older man is less able to influence the attractive young woman with poetry. David Lurie, professor of English, specializes in the Romantic poets—"For as long as he can remember, the harmonies of *The Prelude* have echoed within him" (*D* 13)—and he tries to use Shakespeare to seduce his student Melanie:

"From fairest creatures we desire increase," he says, "that thereby beauty's rose might never die."

Not a good move. Her smile loses its playful, mobile quality. The pentameter, whose cadence once served so well to oil the serpent's words, now only estranges. (*D* 16)

But though it does not bridge this generational gap, he still feels the force of the poetry himself: "Beauty's rose: the poem drives straight as an arrow. She does not own herself; perhaps he does not own himself either" (*D* 18). It takes more than this one rejection by Melanie for him to realize that his love of poetry has not translated into wisdom and that Shakespeare's argument here is hardly the stuff of rational analysis, being an exercise in seduction by rhetoric. However, much later, back in Cape Town, he learns that his successor at the university is "in language learning." He thinks, ruefully, "So much for the poets, so much for the dead masters. Who have not, he must say, guided him well. *Aliter*, to whom he has not listened well" (*D* 179).

Heteroglossia is an inalienable part of David Lurie's consciousness. As John Mullan says, "In reaching for fitting quotations the narrative gives us a sharp sense of his thoughts" (294). Mullan identifies several of the quotations Coetzee uses in *Disgrace*—from Villon, Virgil, Verdi, Goethe, Hardy, Kafka: as he says, "one day an academic editor will identify all the novel's quotations on behalf of toiling students" (295). When David uses the phrase "like a dog" of Lucy's situation, he is quoting from the ending of Kafka's *The Trial*, and *"because we are too menny"* comes from *Jude the Obscure*: it can be deeply instructive to follow these references through at a critical level, as Rita Barnard does in her discussions of the allusion to *Jude the Obscure* and the phrase *das ewig Weibliche*, because they enrich and complicate the possible readings of the novel. There is also a gratification in recognizing the quotations in the narrative, but that is not what they are primarily there for. David Lurie has been formed by the canon of European literature: an alert reader can realize this in a general way without the need to identify every reference. Coetzee himself admits that "I do tend to be allusive, and not always to signal the presence of allusion" ("Roads" 143); it is unlikely that he does this merely to provide an intellectual reward for knowledgeable readers. Nadine Gordimer writes,

> I would...raise an eyebrow at, if not take issue with, critical contention that the difficulties of Coetzee's novels require that the reader shall have read the same books the author has. ... All

literature is a retelling, endlessly, of human life and its ungrasp-
able mysteries, since story-making began. You don't have to know
the provenance to respond to the contemporary version, whether
or not it gives over [*sic*] references. (Preface x–xi)

In *From the Heart of the Country*, Magda sees flying machines in the
sky over her farm and hears messages from them in Spanish:

> I know no Spanish whatsoever. However, it is characteristic of the
> Spanish that is spoken to me out of the flying machines that I find
> it immediately comprehensible. ...
> How can I be deluded when I think so clearly? (*HC* 126)

The rich comedy of Magda's attempts to communicate with these godlike
machines, first by shouting in English, then in her version of Spanish, by
lighting a huge bonfire, then by writing Spanish words with stones, leads
her to the humble admission that "I wish only to be at home in the world
as the merest beast is at home. Much, much less than all would satisfy
me: to begin with, a life unmediated by words" (*HC* 135). Magda, as the
fictional character she is, cannot attain this simple mode of being. She is
nothing but words.

There are two couples in Coetzee's novels who cross cultures and
for whom language differences are felt to be a bar to communication.
In *Waiting for the Barbarians*, the barbarian girl is not at home in the
Magistrate's language: "In the makeshift language we share there are
no nuances. She has a fondness for facts, I note, for pragmatic dicta;
she dislikes fancy, questions, speculations; we are an ill-matched
couple" (*WB* 40). Despite this, however, his inexplicable obsession
with her continues. Paul Rayment, too, is obsessed with a woman
from a somewhat different culture, whose native language he does not
speak:

> [S]he speaks a rapid, approximate Australian English with Slavic
> liquids and an uncertain command of *a* and *the*, coloured by slang
> she must pick up from her children. ... It is a variety of the lan-
> guage he is not familiar with; he rather likes it. (*SM* 27)

But their senses of humor are different, and "their aesthetics are worlds apart" (*SM* 244). Both these relationships with women belonging to other cultures are doomed. (Which, of course, hardly sets them apart from other Coetzee characters: a happy and lasting sexual relationship usually seems beyond their reach.) In *Summertime*, two of the women interviewed feel that their ethnicity is part of their attraction for John. For fellow academic Sophie, John's "Francophilia" contributes to the comic element she retrospectively sees in the relationship, and though she provides very few details of their affair, there is no suggestion that it was unsatisfactory to either. But for Adriana, whom he pursued unsuccessfully, "he was in love with some idea of me, some fantasy of a Latin mistress that he made up in his own mind" (*S* 193–194). Language does not cause their communication difficulties, but she certainly feels that there is a cultural divide:

> If you have fallen in love with a woman, you do not sit down and type her one long letter after another. … But then I thought, perhaps this is how these Dutch Protestants behave when they fall in love: prudently, long-windedly, without fire, without grace. (*S* 172)

The relationships that break down, or never eventuate, fail not only because of linguistic communication difficulties but because the man tends to be guided by his intellect rather than his physical urges.

Titles of books and names of characters play a large part in setting up a reader's expectations. Most of Coetzee's titles are relatively straightforward, *Summertime* being perhaps the most enigmatic. Coming after *Boyhood* and *Youth*, *Summertime* seems to betoken a flourishing time of life, but this is far from the sunny memoir one might be led to expect. Perhaps the title is a joke—only someone from an unpleasantly hot country could describe John's arid existence as "summertime."

The names of characters provide only a little more scope for interpretation. After the flamboyant Eugene Dawn in "The Vietnam Project," Coetzee seems to have largely lost interest in giving his characters distinctive names, and even in using their names very much. Magda's name is not used until page 102 of *From the Heart of the Country*, when it comes up in conversation with Klein-Anna. In this novel, too, there are two Annas. Michael K's mother is also Anna, and J. C.'s love interest in *Diary of a Bad Year* is Anya. He names his cousin Agnes, another variation of Ann, in *Boyhood*, while in *Summertime*, the same character is named Margot. Elizabeth is the Christian name of two of his protagonists. In many of the novels, if characters have names at all, they come from the plainest lexicon of English Christian names: John, Paul, Michael, Susan, David, Alan. In *Slow Man*, oddly, almost all the women have names beginning with M: Marijana, Marianna, Margaret, Madeleine. In *Waiting for the Barbarians*, the main character has no name, and neither does the barbarian girl. Only three characters are named: Joll, Mandel, and Mai, the cook. This plainness is of a piece with Coetzee's spare style in general and can only contribute to the propensity of critics to endow his novels with allegorical meanings.

The names in *The Master of Petersburg* are, of course, heavy with significance from Dostoevsky's life and works. Likewise, in *Foe*, the names Cruso, Foe, and Friday come from *Robinson Crusoe*, while Susan Barton is Coetzee's invention. Perhaps the oddest name in the whole oeuvre is Vercueil: "Vercueil, Verkuil, Verskuil. That's what he says. I have never come across such a name before," says Elizabeth Curren (*AI* 37). In the forest of unremarkable names, a name like this must be significant. A South African telephone directory search reveals that Vercueil is a South African name, though rather uncommon, but that would not prevent a character (or reader) with etymological inclinations from speculating that it is made up of the French words for *worm* and *gather*, appropriate enough for his deathly role in Elizabeth Curren's life. In *Disgrace*, David Lurie thinks about other characters' names—"Bev…a silly name to go by. It reminds me of cattle," he tells Lucy (*D* 79). Bovine, perhaps he is thinking? Lucy forbears from protesting at his snobbishness. But it is his reaction to the name of one of Lucy's attackers that brings on her protest about his irony:

> "The boy you had a row with at Petrus's party. He is staying with Petrus, helping him. His name is Pollux."

> "Not Mncedisi? Not Nqabayakhe? Nothing unpronounceable, just Pollux?"
>
> "P-O-L-L-U-X. And David, can we have some relief from that terrible irony of yours?" (*D* 200)

Pollux, son of Leda and Zeus incarnated as a swan: perhaps an odd name for a South African farm boy. But his relative is Petrus, another Latin name: classical names are not uncommon in this culture. However, Pollux might have an echo in similar though unrelated words like *pollution*, though Lurie never expresses this in his narrative. He does comment on Melanie's name, "Melanie—melody: a meretricious rhyme. Not a good name for her. Shift the accent. Meláni: the dark one" (*D* 18), and also on the name of her sister Desiree, "the desired one: Surely they tempted the gods by giving her a name like that!" (*D* 164). He has himself presumably named his daughter Lucy after Wordsworth's doomed heroine, perhaps also tempting the gods in his own way. Then there are the characters Coetzee has chosen, for various reasons, to give his own surname, in *Dusklands* and, by implication, in *Diary of a Bad Year*. In *Dusklands*, this seems a provocative way to introduce the idea of complicity, while in the later novel, it makes all the more apparently transparent the fictional screen behind which the author stands. The memoirs complicate this fictional screen yet further: it is impossible to know what, beyond his own name, has any basis in fact in these books.

Most of Coetzee's books are centered on writers—potential or actual, amateur or professional. Sometimes the novel, or part of it, is itself the writer's work, like *Dusklands*, *Age of Iron*, and *Foe*. Other books are about writers: *The Master of Petersburg*, *Elizabeth Costello*, and the memoirs. The physical presence of words is essential in his work, and the narratives draw attention to words, sentences, and books as physical objects as well as language and utterances as physical phenomena. From Eugene Dawn's reports to the books of John's Aunt Annie in *Boyhood*, from Magda's verbal self-creation to Elizabeth Costello's frustrating sojourn with Paul Rayment, language and writing are not just implicitly, as they must be with every work of literature, but in an acknowledged and examined way, central to Coetzee's art.

Endnotes

1. Douthwaite, "Coetzee's *Disgrace*" 44. Although in the published text, the word "though" appears, Douthwaite confirmed by e-mail dated 28 June 2007 that "through" is correct.
2. See Coetzee, *In the Heart of the Country*.

Chapter 6

Sex and Desire

Sex is surely a longstanding and insistent preoccupation for Coetzee, so it comes as a surprise to find that it has been the subject of so little critical analysis. Database searches on his name linked with terms like *sex*, *desire*, or *love* yield meager results.[1] Since the majority of the few articles retrieved concern *Disgrace*, in which sex is so prominent a theme, this novel may serve as a starting point for the discussion of various related themes in Coetzee's whole oeuvre.

All these themes appear in *Disgrace*, though with varying degrees of importance, so it may be useful to examine some of the interpretations to which *Disgrace* has given rise in relation to sexual matters, most of which are imbued with a political dimension. John Douthwaite, in his linguistic examination of the first chapter of *Disgrace*, concludes that "the first sentence of the novel is clearly a topical sentence. The topic is announced as being that of sex.... Sex is thus presented as the central topic of the novel" ("Coetzee's *Disgrace*" 43–44). There is a good deal to be learned from the linguistic approach Douthwaite employs: as I showed in chapter 5, his expertise reveals much about Coetzee's precise and skillful deployment of language to convey David Lurie's frame of mind. However, this approach occasionally leads to a literal interpretation which is not necessarily supported by a reading of the novel as a whole, and I am more convinced by Martin Swales' suggestion that "the sexual issue, in its physical, psychological, moral and social dimensions is…not the only—perhaps not even the chief—concern" of *Disgrace* (8).

Although I intend not to focus closely on politics in this study, it would be impossibly limiting to avoid it altogether in relation to sex in Coetzee's work, and in relation to the work of these two scholars, there is one divergence that is particularly telling. As one of a select band of scholars who resist allegorical readings of Coetzee, Swales makes the point that "any attempt to read David's exploitation of Melanie as allegorically expressive of white exploitation of the black population does not carry much conviction—not least because Melanie is white" (9). But is Melanie white? Coetzee fails to make it explicit. In fact, Douthwaite has the opposite view: "I contend that Melanie represents the ultimate step in his [David's] downfall because she is female, young, a student of his, and coloured. In other words, Melanie is defenceless Otherness taken to extremes" ("Melanie" 136). And further:

> Melanie comes from the Greek *melanos*, meaning "black". This establishes ethnic identity, a fact which is confirmed by Lurie when he plays on Melanie's name: "Meláni: the dark one" (18)….[T]he fact that the person is female and black makes the situation far more potentially explosive. ("Melanie" 142)

Douthwaite is in trouble here already by conflating "coloured" and "black," which have quite distinct meanings in the South African context that differ from English or American usage. He compounds this by an overly literal interpretation of the name Melanie. Melanie is described by David as "the dark one," but this could be a reference to her black hair and dark eyes (*D* 11) or might have a more metaphorical connotation. When he meets Melanie's younger sister, David reflects, "Melanie the first born, the dark one, then Desiree, the desired one" (*D* 164), further confirming the unlikelihood of the name Melanie carrying such a literal meaning: if Melanie is dark-skinned, then surely her sister would be too, and this comparison would be meaningless. Naming in Coetzee is never quite as blatant as this. Names are more likely to be appropriate to a character's cultural background—that is, realistic—rather than bearing Bunyanesque or Dickensian connotations, and David's speculation on its etymology is part of Coetzee's development of his character rather than an indication of Melanie's actual characteristics.

Although I am not entirely sure of Melanie's ethnicity, my subjective (and admittedly ignorant, as an Australian who has never lived in South Africa) feeling is that she is not black, that is, of purely African descent, in the way that Petrus and Lucy's attackers are black. To seek clarification, I asked the advice of two South African friends, one of whom reread the novel with my question in mind and told me "I think the student [that is, Melanie] is white" (Lenz). The second opinion was that Melanie was possibly "Cape Coloured," that is, of mixed European and African descent, but definitely not a black African.[2]

This uncertainty is significant because, as can be seen in Douthwaite's article, assumptions like these are frequently used as the basis for constructing allegorical meanings. If Melanie is assumed to be black, a crude symmetry can be set up between David's affair with her and the black men's rape of Lucy. We must presume that Coetzee knows what he is doing: he must realize that his South African readers would have a clearer idea of Melanie's ethnicity than the rest of us, but, as I discovered, even they cannot be absolutely certain. The important point is that he leaves the point open. This cannot be because her color does not matter, and it is unlikely to be an oversight. It is interesting that there is no equivalent doubt amongst critics about Petrus' racial origins, even though it is never explicitly stated that he is black.

When we are introduced to David Lurie, his sexual needs are being fulfilled by the regular services of Soraya. Soraya is certainly colored—her body is "honey-brown" (1)—and a Muslim. David's satisfaction with her is complete:

> It surprises him that ninety minutes a week of a woman's company are enough to make him happy, who used to think he needed

> a wife, a home, a marriage. His needs turn out to be quite light,
> after all, light and fleeting. (*D* 5)

Before Soraya, his sexual history had been one of easily satisfied desire
abruptly curtailed by age:

> With his height, his good bones, his olive skin, his flowing hair,
> he could always count on a degree of magnetism. If he looked at
> a woman in a certain way, with a certain intent, she would return
> his look, he could rely on that. That was how he lived: for years,
> for decades, that was the backbone of his life.
>
> Then one day it all ended. Without warning his powers fled.
> Glances that would once have responded to his slid over, past,
> through him. Overnight he became a ghost. If he wanted a woman
> he had to learn to pursue her; often, in one way or another, to buy
> her.
>
> He existed in an anxious flurry of promiscuity. (*D* 7)

He is able to believe, though on rather doubtful grounds, in Soraya's
affection for him, and thus she is able single-handedly to satisfy his
desire, previously characterized by "anxious" excess, for a year. However, when he encounters her, out of context, with her children, the convenient illusion is broken. As Swales points out, "The novel opens...with
a glimpse of sex that is sustained by an ethos of unalloyed efficiency.
Once that efficiency is disturbed, the possibility of shame emerges—as
both emotional and social reality" (15); shame, which "arises when the
frontiers between distinct and separate worlds are crossed" (11). Once
Soraya becomes unavailable, David is returned to his former state of
anxious desire. Melinda Harvey, drawing on Susan Sontag's character-
ization of the pornographic imagination as tending "to make one person interchangeable with another" (Sontag 53), proceeds to assert that
"it is in this way, then, that Soraya gives way, briefly, to another escort
named 'Soraya', to Dawn, a new secretary from David's department,
and, finally, to...Melanie" (Harvey 101). But, whatever might be said
about the ethics of David's relationship with Soraya, his problem is
precisely that she is not interchangeable. The "new" Soraya—"Soraya

has become, it seems, a popular *nom de commerce*"—is "no more than eighteen, unpractised, to his mind coarse" (*D* 8), and sex with Dawn "is a failure. Bucking and clawing, she works herself into a froth of excitement that in the end only repels him" (*D* 9). Briefly, before the affair with Melanie, he considers dispensing with desire altogether by having himself castrated:

> A simple enough operation surely: they do it to animals every day, and animals survive well enough, if one ignores a certain residue of sadness. Severing, tying off: with local anaesthetic and a steady hand and a modicum of phlegm one might even do it oneself, out of a textbook. A man on a chair snipping away at himself: an ugly sight, but no more ugly, from a certain point of view, than the same man exercising himself on the body of a woman. (*D* 9)

Readings that see David as a thoughtless womanizer tend to ignore this last sentence, the intrusion so early in the novel of a point of view antithetical to that of the sexually predatory male, which is, admittedly, the predominant tone here. In the same way, many readers notice only the "not quite" rape of Melanie (*D* 25) and fail to take account of the consensual sex between them, the "good" times. Lucy Valerie Graham writes, "Although narrative perspective in *Disgrace* allows for critical distance from David Lurie...the majority of reviewers seem to read in sympathy with Lurie when he glosses his sexual encounter with Melanie as 'not rape, not quite that'" (440), whereas "the act that he commits is rape" (438). Not wishing to quibble about definitions, I will accept that the one occasion when "nothing will stop him" (*D* 25) is to all intents and purposes rape. But a week later, she seeks refuge with him, and "he makes love to her one more time":

> It is good, as good as the first time; he is beginning to learn the way her body moves. She is quick, and greedy for experience. … One moment stands out in recollection, when she hooks a leg behind his buttocks to draw him in closer: as the tendon of her inner thigh tightens against him, he feels a surge of joy and desire. (*D* 29)

What are we to make of this? David is not a reliable narrator, but I do not believe we are invited to consider that he is *fabricating* events such as this. His unreliability shows itself in the *interpretation* of the earlier act as "not rape, not quite that," and in his thinking, follow-ing the later act, "Who knows…there might, despite all, be a future" (*D* 29). But the *fact* of this act of consensual sex is not subject to unreli-able narration: if it were, the whole narrative would lose its integrity. If, as Harvey believes, "Coetzee is at least provoking us to think of Melanie's 'undesired' seduction…in terms of the European colonisation of Africa" (103), how is he prompting us to think of consensual sex? If one episode can provoke an allegorical interpretation, why not the other? Harvey admits that it is "difficult to unravel…whether David's sexual misdemeanours are playing mirror or foil to his daughter Lucy's rape later on in the novel," and that "Coetzee is not for one minute inter-ested in stitching up an answer to this question for us" (103). It is hard to ignore the evidence that Melanie has far more ambivalent feelings towards David than Lucy has to her attackers, and it is surely patroniz-ing to regard this young woman as an entirely passive victim, although she is, David realizes, "[t]oo young. She will not know how to deal with him; he ought to let her go" (*D* 18). However limited and unequal in power, there is some mutual feeling between them. But, as J. C. writes in *Diary of a Bad Year*,

> As for sex between teachers and students, so strong is the tide of disapproval nowadays that uttering even the mildest word in its defence becomes (exactly) like battling that tide, feeling your puny stroke quite overwhelmed by a great heft of water bearing you backward. What you face when you open your lips to speak is not the silencing stroke of the censor but an edict of exile. (*DBY* 48)

Until Anya reads this essay, "On Paedophilia," she thinks J. C. is harm-less: "For an old man, after all, what is there left in the world but wicked thoughts? Señor C can't help it if he desires me, just as I can't help it if I am desired" (*DBY* 70). Now, however, she wonders "if I have misjudged him all along" (*DBY* 71). But there is nothing in the novel to support this idea, and it seems that it is merely an example of the very "tide of disapproval" he is discussing.

Although we discover nothing about the thoughts of Lucy's rapists, it must be safe to assume, within the scheme of the novel, that they are not indulging in reflections like David's:

> She is behaving badly, getting away with too much; she is learning to exploit him and will probably exploit him further. But if she has got away with much, he has got away with more; if she is behaving badly, he has behaved worse. To the extent that they are together, if they are together, he is the one who leads, she the one who follows. Let him not forget that. (*D* 28)

Further, David's seduction of Melanie is founded on his desire particularly for her, sexual desire which he knows involves him in greater risk than her: as Swales points out, "she has allies and defenders who ensure that the university system, sensitive as it is to any whiff of sexual impropriety, swiftly punishes David" (9). Melanie, as we discover later in the novel, "has resumed her studies. ... She is going on with theatre work in her spare time, and doing well" (*D* 166), and when David sees her on stage, his perception is that

> she is altogether more sure of herself than before…Is it possible that in the months he has been away she has grown up, found herself? *Whatever does not kill me makes me stronger.* Perhaps the trial was a trial for her too; perhaps she too has suffered, and come through. (*D* 191)

Point of view cannot be discounted, of course: this may be wishful thinking on David's part. Nevertheless, it at least demonstrates some measure of concern for Melanie's welfare, however compromised. Lucy's rapists, on the other hand, perpetrate an act of violent hatred against a woman presumably chosen not for her particular desirableness but for her race and vulnerability, and she is badly damaged by the attack. There are many who will regard this distinction as untenable: rape is rape, they will say, and no one instance can be more excusable than another. Graham, for example, believes that

> [i]t is important to acknowledge that the novel dissolves clear boundaries of identity between Lurie and the men who rape Lucy. Like these men, Lurie is also a rapist and (albeit in a different way) a dog-killer. ... [And] the stories of Melanie and Lucy are elided. (443–444)

There is, as she acknowledges, a qualitative difference in their modes of dog-killing (in which case, it seems trivial to bring it up), but not in their modes of raping, or in Melanie and Lucy's experience of undesired sex. David himself "thinks of Byron. Among the legions of countesses and kitchenmaids Byron pushed himself into there were no doubt those who called it rape. But none surely had cause to fear that the session would end with her throat being slit" (*D* 160). Should we also equate Melanie's return to David with Lucy's resignation to the possibility that her rapists might come back? There seems little point in reading complex and nuanced narratives such as *Disgrace* if such crude parallels are to be drawn. As Swales says,

> Admittedly there are intimations of grand allegory to which the names of the characters contribute: Lucy is the source of light and fruitful tiller of the soil, the white woman bearing the child of the coloured man who puts herself under the protection of Petrus, the rock of the new order. Yet any such allegory is crass and absurd, an offence to both moral and historical logic. The closing cadence of the novel is much more understated and simply registers the continuance of life and death, earthiness and consciousness, brutality and compassion. (19)

David's admission that he can understand what it feels like to be a rapist, that he "can, if he concentrates, if he loses himself, be there, be the men, inhabit them, fill them with the ghost of himself" (*D* 160) is surely a step towards the shaky redemption he seeks rather than a further sign of his culpability, especially when he then wonders, "[D]oes he have it in him to be the woman?" (*D* 160).

Sexual desire contributes to David Lurie's downfall, and in different ways, it troubles many of Coetzee's characters. In *Boyhood*, John "likes to gaze at slim, smooth brown legs in tight shorts":

> Beauty and desire: he is disturbed by the feelings that the legs of these boys, blank and perfect and inexpressive, create in him. What is there that can be done with legs beyond devouring them with one's eyes? What is desire *for*?
>
> The naked sculptures in the *Children's Encyclopaedia* affect him in the same way: Daphne pursued by Apollo; Persephone ravished by Dis. It is a matter of shape, of perfection of shape. He has an idea of the perfect human body. When he sees that perfection manifested in white marble, something thrills inside him; a gulf opens up; he is on the edge of falling.
>
> Of all the secrets that set him apart, this may in the end be the worst. Among all these boys he is the only one in whom this dark erotic current runs; among all this innocence and normality, he is the only one who desires. (*B* 56–57)

Magda, in *From the Heart of the Country*, similarly asks herself, "What does one do with desire?" Unlike the young John, however, she feels no shame coupled with her desire and can form some kind of answer:

> I feel like…a great emptiness, an emptiness filled with a great absence, an absence which is a desire to be filled, to be fulfilled. Yet at the same time I know that nothing will fill me, because it is the first condition of life forever to desire, otherwise life would cease. It is a principle of life forever to be unfulfilled. Fulfilment does not fulfil. (*HC* 114)

This discourse of desire and frustration is directed towards the current object of Magda's desire, the servant Anna, but it is useless as a means of seduction:

> This is what she gets from me, colonial philosophy, words with no history behind them, homespun, when she wants stories. … But these words of mine come from nowhere and go nowhere, they have no past or future, they whistle across the flats in a desolate eternal present, feeding no one. (*HC* 115)

In *Doubling the Point*, Coetzee says, "[I]t is not productive to discover the answer to the question of why one desires: the answer threatens the end of desire, the end of the production of desire" (*DP* 207–208). The Magistrate in *Waiting for the Barbarians* is unable to answer the question. "I am with her not for whatever raptures she may promise or yield but for other reasons, which remain as obscure to me as ever" (*WB* 64). At the point when he is about to hand the barbarian girl back to her people, he asks her to return to live with him:

> "Do you understand me? That is what I want."
> "Why?" The word falls with deathly softness from her lips. She knows that it confounds me, has confounded me from the beginning. (*WB* 71)

Despite his earlier "fury of disbelief" at the notion of the parallels between his behavior and that of Colonel Joll (*WB* 44), the nearest he can come to an explanation is that his desire was counterfeit:

> She must have felt a miasma of deceit closing about her: envy, pity, cruelty all masquerading as desire...I was the lie that Empire tells itself when times are easy, [Joll] the truth that Empire tells when harsh winds blow. Two sides of imperial rule, no more, no less. (*WB* 135)

His self-deception, his whole attitude towards the girl, had been "a year of confused and futile gestures of expiation" (*WB* 135). His desire, rather than being genuine desire which retreats before the questions of its own origins, finally seems to have yielded its meaning to him after all his self-questioning, and it is, despite everything, a political one.

Desire is never simple and usually has a dark side. Fyodor in *The Master of Petersburg* feels "an unexpected flutter of desire" for the tall girl who is actually Nechaev in disguise, a feeling that "disturbs him" at the time (*MP* 98) and in retrospect is revealed as all the more troubling when he discovers the deception, and he wonders with disgust...[how] Pavel could have been friends with people like these, people ever-eager to whip themselves into frenzies of self-righteousness?...Extremists all of them, sensualists hungering for the ecstasy of death—killing, dying, no matter which. (*MP* 104–105)

Fyodor desires Anna Sergeyevna in an adult, equal way: "More than the tug of the body, he feels what he can only call kinship with her" (*MP* 63), but he is troubled by an insistent question: "Loving the mother, is one destined to long for the daughter too?" (*MP* 128). Anna feels this tension too: "You use me as a route to my child," she accuses (*MP* 231). He protests, "I would not lay a finger on her, I swear," to which she responds, "It has nothing to do with *laying fingers*, as you well know" (*MP* 232). And indeed, his "assault upon the innocence" of Matryona is achieved through writing rather than a physical act. In *Summertime*, too, there is a suggestion in Adriana's interview that John's one-sided passion for her is really a way to her daughter: "Even when I was alone with him I would have been thinking, *It is not me he desires, it is Maria Regina, who is young and beautiful but is forbidden to him*" (*S* 192), and she worries that the poetry (Keats' "Ode to Melancholy") he is introducing to her daughter is fostering her "romantic dreams" (*S* 158).

In *Youth*, rather than being gripped by inconvenient and inappropriate desires like aging characters such as Fyodor, the Magistrate, and David Lurie, John seems more troubled by its absence. "He believes in passionate love and its transfiguring power. His experience, however, is that amatory relations devour his time, exhaust him, and cripple his work" (*Y* 78). Though "[a]s a student he was in a continual fever of lovesickness, now for one girl, now for another, sometimes for two at the same time" (*Y* 79), and he dreams of European film stars, confronted with a real woman, he is cold, awkward, and inept. Even when naked in bed with a girl from a poetry group, though "[h]e marvels at the shapeliness of her naked body, the ivory whiteness of her skin...there is no warmth between them; and warmth, it becomes clear, will not grow" (*Y* 73). He seems hardly to have progressed from the "new, ugly self" he became at thirteen, "embarrassed all the time...like a crab pulled out of its shell, pink and wounded and obscene" (*B* 151). John, in *Summertime*, is described by various women as cold, "autistic" (*S* 52), timid, wooden, inhuman, "not a sensual being" (*S* 193). The biggest puzzle in this book is that it is so obsessed with John's sexual affairs. Martin questions Vincent about the witnesses he has chosen to interview for his biography: "[W]as either of the women you mentioned emotionally involved with Coetzee?" When Vincent replies in the affirmative, Martin rejoins:

> Shouldn't that give you pause? Are you not inevitably going to come out with an account that is slanted toward the personal and the intimate at the expense of the man's actual achievements as a writer?...Because it is not in the nature of love affairs for the lovers to see each other whole and steady. (*S* 218)

Vincent has nothing to say in response, frustratingly, because this is a question which must have occurred to every reader. Perhaps, as I suggested in chapter 3, it is a slap on the wrist for the over-inquisitive. Or perhaps it is an acknowledgment that the writer, however intellectual, is embodied, and the published oeuvre comes from a feeling, suffering human being, in this case, one who seems to have had little idea how to conduct intimate relationships.

Other young men in Coetzee have similar difficulties. Michael K "had never known how to behave with women," and a rare episode of sexual desire is for a girl in the camp whose baby has died. He watches her in her grief, immobile and refusing food and consolation.

> K wondered whether he was at last in love. Then after three days the girl re-emerged and resumed her life. Seeing her in the midst of other people, K could detect no sign that she was different from them. He never spoke to her. (*MK* 89)

Later, at Sea Point after his escape from the reeducation camp, he is seduced by one of the women he meets, remaining passive throughout:

> She bent down and took his penis in her mouth. He wanted to push her off but his fingers recoiled from the stiff dead hair of the

wig. So he relaxed, allowing himself to be lost in the spinning inside his head and in the faraway wet warmth. (*MK* 178–179)

Thinking about the episode later, he reflects, "I have become an object of charity" (*MK* 181). The call of the flesh, for Michael, is weak and always regarded with detachment; shortly after the woman seduces him, he sees some girls at the beach: "He watched their backsides ascend the steps and surprised in himself an urge to dig his fingers into that soft flesh" (*MK* 180). As with the girl in the camp who made him "wonder whether he was at last in love" (*MK* 89), he is divided intellectually from the side of him that desires almost as much as John in *Youth*, and his feelings seem more theoretical and experimental than elemental. And, of course, the desires of the appalling Eugene in *Dusklands* are perverted: sexual relations with his wife are a constant source of disappointment (all her fault, of course), but "I sometimes think that I might climb to the highest pitch of ecstasy if only Marilyn would sleep though the sexual business" (*DL* 12). He finds his fantasies of her unfaithfulness make her "so much the dearer to me, for if strangers prize her she must be valuable" (*DL* 11). Meanwhile, his collection of photographs of atrocities visited upon the Vietnamese by American soldiers can be

> relied upon to give my imagination the slight electric impulse that is all it needs to set it free again. … I tremble and sweat, my blood pounds, I am unstrung and fit this night only for shallow, bilious sleep. Surely, I whisper to myself, if they arouse me like this I am a man and these images of phantoms a subject fit for men! (*DL* 13, 15)

However, in the end, it is not Eugene's sexual desires that trigger his pathological behavior. In general, Coetzee's young male characters, then, tend not to be ruled by sexual desire, even though they might wish to be.

The activity of desire in the aging body seems to be of more interest to Coetzee. In *Waiting for the Barbarians*, the Magistrate spent his youth prowling the town wearing "the well-fed look of a prize boar" (*WB* 45), but approaching middle age, he started to feel, like several other of Coetzee's characters, that "[d]esire seemed to bring with it a pathos of distance and separation which it was futile to deny" (*WB* 45). Desire, here, seems to carry within it, in the aging mind, the seeds of its own demise.

Many critics regard *Disgrace* as being "about" sex. According to Harvey, "For proof that sex is a real subject of *Disgrace*, we need only turn to the novel's first page" (99), and Douthwaite, as I have mentioned, claims that, since sex is the subject of the novel's first sentence, "[s]ex is thus presented as the central topic of the novel" ("Coetzee's *Disgrace*" 44). However, it may be significant that age is mentioned before sex in that first sentence: "For a man of his age, fifty-two, divorced, he has, to his mind, solved the problem of sex rather well" (*D* 1), and after the failed episodes with Soraya's successors and before Melanie, David Lurie contemplates "retir[ing] from the game" (*D* 9). Later, watching Melanie on stage from the auditorium, he ponders:

> An unseemly business, sitting in the dark spying on a girl (unbidden the world *letching* comes to him). Yet the old men whose company he seems to be on the point of joining, the tramps and drifters with their stained raincoats and cracked false teeth and hairy earholes—all of them were once upon a time children of God, with straight limbs and clear eyes. Can they be blamed for clinging to the last to their place at the sweet banquet of the senses? (*D* 24)

Fifty-two seems young to be contemplating "the proper business of the old: preparing to die" (*D* 9): an aspect, perhaps, of David's melodramatic attitude to himself and his own concerns. However, the injuries he suffers in the attack on the farm when Lucy is raped confirm his feeling that he has come, in Byronic terms, to the "end of roving" (*D* 120). After sex with Bev Shaw, he is chastened, his self-image as a great lover shattered:

> Let me not forget this day, he tells himself, lying beside her when they are spent. After the sweet young flesh of Melanie Isaacs, this is what I have come to. This is what I will have to get used to, this and even less than this. ...

His thoughts go to Emma Bovary strutting before the mirror after her first big afternoon. *I have a lover! I have a lover!* sings Emma to herself. Well, let poor Bev Shaw go home and do some singing too. And let him stop calling her poor Bev Shaw. If she is poor, he is bankrupt. (*D* 150)

It is a sign of David's faltering movement towards a calmer, less self-absorbed maturity that, their sexual relationship over, the novel ends with him occupied companionably with Bev in their difficult task of mercy-killing, having learned from her to give the dogs "what he no longer has difficulty in calling by its proper name: love" (*D* 219). He might not love Bev Shaw, but that he can learn from her in this way indicates some level of engagement, and it is also telling that he can "find it in his heart to love" Byron's middle-aged former lover Teresa, "this plain ordinary woman" (*D* 182).

Of course sex *is* one of the topics of *Disgrace*, inasmuch as one can talk of topics in art, but it is interwoven with other, equally strong themes, including not only the politics of South Africa but also the acceptance, however grudging, of the onset of old age and the inevitability of death. *Diary of a Bad Year* shows a more graceful acceptance of aging and death, with the elderly J. C., twenty years older than David Lurie, refraining from any attempt to seduce Anya, despite her "beauty and freshness." In fact, his courtesy and respect for her do seduce her in a way: she leaves the amoral Alan, and she vows to be with J. C. on his deathbed, to "give him a kiss on the brow, a proper kiss, just to remind him of what he is leaving behind" (*DBY* 178).

Another Coetzee character who has trouble with inconvenient desires in later life is Paul Rayment in *Slow Man*, although at first he is immune to the "gross desires" he is expected to feel towards his nurses: "being a lecherous old goat is part of the game, a game he is declining to play" (*SM* 14). Asked by his friend Margaret whether he has "decided this is the end of [his] sexual life," he wonders, "What if the snorting black steed of passion has given up the ghost? The twilight of his manhood. What a letdown; but what a relief too!" (*SM* 57). However, it is not long before he is smitten by Marijana and has become more willing to play the game than his nurse finds comfortable or convenient. "No demand?" she responds to his claim that he makes no demands on her. "You think I know nothing about men? Men is always demand" (*SM* 211). At their most intimate moment, she is giving him a massage, and it is "all one to him, one movement: the swelling of the soul, the swelling of the heart, the swelling of desire. He cannot imagine loving God more than he loves Marijana at this moment" (*SM* 186). But his bliss is interrupted by the appearance of Marijana's young daughter, staring severely at him, "old and ugly and hairy and half naked and no doubt to her angelic nostrils smelly, wrestling with her mother, the two of them trapped in a posture that does not even have the repulsive majesty of intercourse" (*SM* 187–188). The objective gaze undermines the intense subjective pleasure of sensuality. He later begins to wonder about the plausibility of his disinterested love for Marijana:

> Marijana is wearing blue plastic sandals. Blue sandals and purple toenails: he may be an ex-portrait photographer and Marijana may be an ex-picture restorer, but their aesthetics are worlds apart. Very likely other things about them are worlds apart too. Their attitude towards mine and thine, for instance. A woman he had dreamed of prising away from her husband…what would it be like in reality, looking after her and her two hostile daughters and her treacherous son? How long would he last, he and his protective wing? On the other hand…On the other hand, how proud her breasts, how comely! (*SM* 244)

The pull of the erotic against all that is sensible is expressed neatly in this last sentence. Similarly, David Lurie reflects, "He has always been drawn to women of wit. Wit and beauty. With the best will in the world he could not find wit in Meláni. But plenty of beauty" (*D* 78). In *Diary of a Bad Year*, J. C. starts out initially by expressing snobbish opinions about Anya's schooling: "She speaks French with an accent the French probably find charming but has not heard of Voltaire" (*DBY* 60). In this case, though, these opinions occur early in their friendship:

> While I had a very clear sense of her physical being, both as it was now and as it would be in the future, as one might have the clearest

sense of a flower—its radiance, it brave upthrust, its weight in the world—I had no real grasp of what went on in the mind of this woman with whom—out of my own boredom, no doubt, my own idleness, my own empty-headedness—I seem to have grown obsessed, to the extent that a man can be called obsessed when the sexual urge has dwindled and there is only a hovering uncertainty about what he is actually after, what he expects the object of his infatuation to supply. (*DBY* 71–72)

He later develops more respect for Anya, and it is mutual. In a strange way, they have a future together, though he is dying, whereas Paul has no future with Marijana. She even suggests that they might "in another life" have set up house together (*DBY* 159), and she is quite candid about her sexuality and the way she uses it: "[W]hen I make my silky moves I can feel his eyes lock onto me. That is the game between him and me. I don't mind. What else is your bottom for? Use it or lose it" (*DBY* 25). The tendency of *Diary of a Bad Year* is in the opposite direction from the earlier novels where a loner becomes increasingly alone, and though he or she may find a companion, it is never a soul mate. What is not clear is whether this makes this novel any better as a work of art. Is there not the slightest hint of wishful thinking about the whole novel, in Anya's increasing devotion to this elderly man who is so easily identified with the author?

Acts of sexual charity find their way into several Coetzee novels, and usually there is considerable ambivalence involved. Susan Barton, though initially resisting Cruso's advances, thinks, "He has not known a woman for fifteen years, why should he not have his desire?" (*F* 30) and cannot decide whether or not it is a cause of regret:

> We yield to a stranger's embrace or give ourselves to the waves; for the blink of an eyelid our vigilance relaxes; we are asleep; and when we awake we have lost the direction of our lives. What are these blinks of an eyelid, against which the only defence is an eternal and inhuman wakefulness? Might they not be the cracks and chinks through which another voice, other voices, speak in our lives? By what right do we close our ears to them? (*F* 30)

David Lurie and Bev Shaw, Paul Rayment and Marianne: in each of these couples, both parties probably believe that the charity lies on their side, but David and Paul are at least aware that the other also thinks so. There is no future for either of these sexual pairings. Or, of course, for the forty-year-old Elizabeth Costello's act of *caritas* performed on old Mr. Phillips in his last days; she presents it, many years later, in the letter she will not send to her sister, as indubitably that:

> From the swelling of her heart she knows it, from the utter, illim-
> itable difference between what is in her heart and what Nurse
> Naidoo would see, if by some mischance Nurse Naidoo, using her
> pass key, were to fling open the door and stride in. (*EC* 154)

But, like Susan, she wonders, "What can one make of episodes like this, unforeseen, unplanned, out of character? Are they just holes, holes in the heart, into which one steps and falls and then goes on falling?" (*EC* 155). Michael K silently resents the charity forced on him by the woman in the blond wig. How can we say that this woman is not equally filled with Christian *caritas* as Costello, or that Mr. Phillips does not also feel a little rebellious when she is "withdrawing and covering [him] up and giving him a smile and patting his hand" (*EC* 154)?

But what comes of desire in Coetzee's world? As the young John asks, "What is desire *for*?" (*B* 56). In *Foe*, Susan hopefully asks,

> Who would venture to say that what passes between lovers is of
> substance (I refer to their lovemaking, not their talk), yet is it not
> true that something is passed between them, back and forth, and
> they come away refreshed and healed for a while of their loneli-
> ness? (*F* 96–97)

Nevertheless, enduring or even briefly happy relationships are rare in Coetzee's books. Marriages, from Eugene and Marilyn Dawn—"Marilyn was certainly my worst mistake," says Eugene (*DL* 44)—to John's parents in *Boyhood*, to David Lurie's two failed attempts, seem doomed. Though Coetzee's biography lists a marriage to Philippa Jubber in 1963, with two children born in 1966 and 1968 (The Nobel Foundation), this marriage is not mentioned at all in *Summertime*, set in 1972–1975; John behaves like a single man throughout the book. His cousin Margot has a good marriage, but both Julia and Sophie are unhappily married, while Adriana's husband is dying in a hospital at the time she knows John. In the background of some novels, there is occasionally a well-matched couple: Bev and Bill Shaw, perhaps, might fare well enough if her brief fling with David does not ruin things—perhaps Bill would regard it as David feels Bev does, as an act of charity—and despite all, Marijana's final appearance in *Slow Man* shows Paul that her marriage is "an intimate relationship with a row every now and again, Balkan style, to add a dash of spice" (*SM* 253). When Fyodor returns to his young wife, Anna, after his affair with Anna Sergeyevna, he thinks she

> will be changed, will be infused with the trace he will bring back of this subtle, sensually gifted widow. ... He wonders what his wife would think. His indiscretions hitherto have been followed by remorse and, on the heels of remorse, a voluptuous urge to confess. These confessions, tortured in expression yet vague in point of detail, have confused and infuriated his wife, bedevilling their marriage far more than the infidelities themselves. (*MP* 60, 62)

Disgrace, oddly, ends in an engagement, but one unlike anything dreamt of in romantic comedy. As Lucy points out, "Petrus is not offering me a church wedding followed by a honeymoon on the Wild Coast. He is offering an alliance, a deal. I contribute the land, in return for which I am allowed to creep in under his wing" (*D* 203). And Magda has a vision of marriage comic in its ghastliness:

> I have been able, sometimes for days on end, to lose my sense of election, to see myself as simply a lonely, ugly old maid, capable of redemption, to some extent, from loneliness, from loneness, by marriage, a human institution, to another lone soul, a soul perhaps greedier than most, stupider, uglier, not much of a catch, but then what kind of catch am I; whom I would vow to bend to a little lower, slave for a little harder than another woman would, whom I would have to disrobe for on Saturday nights, in the dark, so as not to alarm him, and arouse, if the arts of arousal can be learned, and

> guide to the right hold, rendered penetrable with a gob of chick-
> enfat from the pot at the bedside, and endure the huffing and puff-
> ing of, and be filled eventually, one expects, with seed by, and lie
> listening to the snoring of, till the balm of slumber arrive. What I
> lack in experience I plainly make up for in vision; if the commerce
> of men with women is not like that it might as well be. (*HC* 42)

So desire is not, in Coetzee's world, a force that often leads to com-
panionate affairs or marriages, even when it deepens into love. In fact,
desire is something to be dealt with as efficiently as possible. David
Lurie begins by contemplating his opera heroine Teresa, but his attention
soon moves to himself:

> A woman in love, wallowing in love; a cat on a roof, howling;
> complex proteins swirling in the blood, distending the sexual
> organs, making the palms sweat and voice thicken as the soul
> hurls its longings to the skies. That is what Soraya and the others
> were for: to suck the complex proteins out of his blood like snake-
> venom, leaving him clear-headed and dry. (*D* 185)

When David picks up a streetwalker and she has "done her work on
him…he feels drowsy, contented. … *So this is all it takes!*, he thinks.
How could I ever have forgotten it?" (*D* 194) The Magistrate in *Waiting
for the Barbarians*, in younger days, felt ruled by his imperious desires:

> Sometimes my sex seemed to me another being entirely, a stu-
> pid animal living parasitically upon me, swelling and dwindling
> according to autonomous appetites, anchored to my flesh with
> claws I could not detach. Why do I have to carry you about from
> woman to woman, I asked: simply because you were born with-
> out legs? (*WB* 45–46)

After his ordeal at the hands of Joll, when normality has begun to return
to the town, he asks an herbalist for a potion to subdue his "sex," which
"begins to reassert itself":

> "But tell me," he says, "why should a fine healthy man like your-
> self want to kill off his desires?"

> "It has nothing to do with desire, father. It is simply an irrita-
> tion. A stiffening. Like rheumatism." (*WB* 150)

He has a brief affair with Mai, the cook at the inn, and afterwards, "[f]or
an evening or two I experience a quiet, fickle sadness, before I begin to
forget" (*WB* 153). Desire has been dealt with, and there is nothing left:
he feels "like a man who lost his way long ago but presses on along a
road that may lead nowhere" (*WB* 156). As Magda says, "[I]t is the first
condition of life forever to desire, otherwise life would cease" (*HC* 114).
For the Magistrate, there is little left which can be called *life* rather than
mere *existence*.

In her lesson 7, on "Eros," Elizabeth Costello talks of love and
death and the envy the immortals have for mortal humans: the frisson
that they cannot feel in the act of sex, the "inimitable little quiver"
(*EC* 189). In *Foe*, the approach of death makes Cruso more passionate, and, as the Magistrate says, "We all know, what old men seek is
to recover their youth in the arms of young women" (*WB* 128). There
is a strong implication in *Disgrace* that David is trying to do just that,
and Paul in *Slow Man* as well. It hardly needs saying that these efforts
are futile, but for Coetzee, they seem to be a recurring subject worth
exploring. J. C. in *Diary of a Bad Year*, however, seeks in Anya not
so much the recovery of lost youth as consolation for the approach of
death. Elizabeth Costello finds it "[s]trange how, as desire relaxes its
grip on her body, she sees more and more clearly a universe ruled by
desire" (*EC* 191):

> Or if *desire* is still too rude a word, then what of *appetency*?
> Appetency and chance: a powerful duo, more than powerful
> enough to build a cosmology on, from the atoms and the little
> things with nonsense names that make up atoms to Alpha Cen-
> tauri and Cassiopeia and the great dark back of beyond. The gods
> and ourselves, whirled helplessly around by the winds of chance,
> yet pulled equally towards each other. ... Not the least thing, not
> the last thing but is called to by love. (*EC* 192)

Of course, speaking less metaphysically, desire is *for* the begetting of children, and the love between parents and their children is, in Coetzee's novels, a more enduring bond, though frequently no less troubled. This bond is the subject of my next chapter.

ENDNOTES

1. For example, the search "Coetzee" in Person—About AND "(sex or desire or love)" as keywords in the MLA international database, performed on 2 October 2009, yielded sixteen articles, three of which are irrelevant, the keyword having been used in an unrelated context. The search "Coetzee" in Person—About with no qualifying keywords generates 726 hits.
2. Shlomowitz. The 2008 Steve Jacobs film of Disgrace cast Antoinette Engel, a colored woman, as Melanie. It remains to be seen what effect this (and other aspects of the film) will have on interpretations of the novel.

CHAPTER 7

PARENTS AND CHILDREN

Many of Coetzee's characters, despite their alienation and solitude, are part of a family, however sketchy or partial. Within the scheme of each novel, there are never more than two or three family members who are significant in the main character's life during the novel's action; often there is only one, sometimes none. Paola Splendore points out that "most of Coetzee's characters are not only primarily introduced in terms of their family status, but the plots of the novels often revolve around family ties and obligations" (150). However, few of his characters are married, though they are often divorced, and very few have brothers or sisters. Indeed, it is quite remarkable how absent the link, either comradely or combative, between siblings is from his work. In *Boyhood*, there is a younger brother who leaves very little impression: the book reads like a memoir of an only child. Likewise, in *Summertime*, Julia is surprised when she discovers John has a brother because he "has the air of an only child" (*S* 46). The brother is hardly mentioned elsewhere in the book. The only other sibling of a main character who plays a part in any of the books is Blanche in *Elizabeth Costello*, who appears only in the one "lesson" on "The Humanities in Africa"; it is a characteristic of this novel that consistent realistic elements are not introduced merely for verisimilitude, but only when they are needed for a particular purpose. In any event, it is clear that the lateral family bond is of little interest to Coetzee, whereas the intergenerational bond is frequently of great significance, either parent to child, or child to parent, or both. Characters who have no children often seek substitute children. For characters whose parents feature in the narrative, the bond is often strong but fraught with ambivalence and conflict.

In *Slow Man*, Paul Rayment bemoans the decline in the size of families in Western societies:

> His grandparents Rayment had six children. His parents had two. He has none. Six, two, one or none: all around him he sees the miserable sequence repeated. He used to think it made sense in an overpopulated world, childlessness was surely a virtue, like peaceableness, like forbearance. Now, on the contrary, childlessness looks to him like madness, a herd madness, even a sin. (*SM* 34)

The lament about childlessness recurs throughout *Slow Man* like a leitmotif. "What could be more selfish, more miserly, than dying childless, terminating the line, subtracting oneself from the great work of generation? Worse than miserly, in fact: unnatural" (*SM* 20). "He has many regrets, he is full of regrets, they come back nightly like roosting birds. Chief among them is regret that he does not have a son" (*SM* 44). Rayment is an outsider who has been beset by an urge to become an insider: he has no children, but now he wants to remedy that omission. The desire to parent a child is at one stage expressed in terms of feminine longings which are at odds with the male sex drive, so it appears that this is a stronger motivation for his actions, almost, than sex itself: "He is like a woman who, having never borne a child, having grown too old for it, now hungers suddenly and urgently for motherhood. Hungry enough to steal another's child: it is as mad as that" (*SM* 73). As he explains to Elizabeth Costello,

> Before it is too late I would like to perform some act that will be—excuse the word—a blessing, however modest, on the lives of others. Why, you ask? Ultimately, because I have no child of

my own to bless as a father does. Having no child was the great
mistake of my life. (*SM* 155)

His attraction to the Jokic family begins with his desire for Marijana, but
it soon broadens to include the children as well. He sets out to become
a benefactor to the Jokics—"to be father to these excellent, beautiful
children and husband to Marijana—co-father if need be, co-husband if
need be, platonic if need be" (*SM* 72): he is prepared to forego sex in
return for the privileges of parenthood. He offers to pay the expensive
fees for Drago's boarding school; he buys off the jewelry store that has
threatened to charge Blanka with shoplifting. Inevitably, though, when
Drago starts to take advantage of his generosity, disillusionment sets
in. He complains to Elizabeth Costello, echoing every parent since the
beginning of time, "[W]hat upsets me is the way he reacts when I dare to
ask for a little consideration" (*SM* 181). Later, contemplating Marijana's
purple toenails, he wonders, "[W]hat would it be like in reality, looking
after her and her two hostile daughters and her treacherous son? How
long would he last, he and his protective wing?" (*SM* 244). At the end
of the novel, we are left in doubt as to whether the relationship with the
Jokics will continue. Costello thinks not: "Sunday may well mark the
last of your dealings with the Jokics, Mrs Jokic included" (*SM* 260). He
seems to have more or less accepted this himself: "Half an hour ago he
was with Marijana. But Marijana is behind them now, and he is left with
Elizabeth Costello" (*SM* 263). He firmly but politely sends her away,
and that is that. He is alone once more with the prospect of a lonely but
untroubled old age. Despite his anguished longing, he does not take the
kind of decisive action Costello wishes him to, either from caution, or
because he is perversely intent on resisting her urgings.

   In *Diary of a Bad Year*, J. C. tells Anya that "children are a gift from
above. It appears I did not merit the gift" (*DBY* 49). However, later, he
wryly notes,

> I approve of children, in the abstract. Children are our future. It is
> good for old people to be around children, it lifts our spirits. And
> so forth.

> What I forget about children is the unending racket they make.
> (*DBY* 167)

So, although J. C. regrets that he has had no children, his longing is not as acute as Paul Rayment's and does not result in even the mild and temporary complications and embarrassment Rayment experiences. However, it is notable that his jealousy of Anya's boyfriend is stimulated not so much by the fact of their sexual relationship but by the possibility of procreation, which he brings up in conversation:

> So you have no plans for children.
>   No. Alan doesn't want children.
>   There is an innocent, a purely sociable, an even routine way of raising the question of children. At the moment when I pronounce the first word, the word *So*, my curiosity could not be more innocent. But in between *So* and the second word *you* the devil waylays me, sends me an image of this Anya on a sweaty summer night, convulsed in the arms of ginger-haired, freckle-shouldered Alan, opening her womb in gladness to the gush of his male juices. (*DBY* 44–46)

Unlike Rayment, J. C. succeeds, in a way, in gaining a child. At the end of her narrative, Anya pledges to act as a child would to a parent, rather than a mistress to her lover, upon J. C.'s death:

> I will clean up afterwards. I will clean your flat and put everything in order. I will drop *Russian Dolls* and the other private stuff in the trash, so you don't need to have sinking thoughts on the other side about what people on this side will be saying about you. I will take your clothes to the charity shop. (*DBY* 177)

This has not been a lifelong preoccupation with Coetzee, however. In the early novels, childlessness is not a matter of regret, and indeed, the existence of a child can be troublesome. Eugene Dawn's feelings towards his son Martin are confused in the extreme. He refers to him as his wife's child—"her child" rather than "mine" or "ours" (*DL* 8)—but then abducts him. The child behaves well at first: "With me Martin is

quite the little man. He is proud of his father and wishes to be like him,"
(*DL* 35), but after four days, he

> is beginning to whine…He wants to know when we are going
> home. … How loud must I shout, how wide with passion must
> my eyes glare, how must my hands shake before he will believe
> that all is for the best, that I love him with a father's love, that I
> desire only that he should grow to be what I am not, a happy man?
> (*DL* 37–38)

The appalling comedy of a fretful, frightened child subjected to the rage
of his father attempting to demonstrate his love is yet another example
of Eugene's irrational, self-centered, and confused approach to life in
general and family love in particular. The ambivalence culminates in his
attack on Martin in the motel room. Afterwards, under therapy, Eugene
claims to

> look back with pleasurable nostalgia to our walks in the woods.
> His childish laughter still echoes in my ears. I think he loved me,
> then. I am sorry for what I did to him. I am sorry but not guilty:
> because I know that if Martin understood the strain I was under he
> would forgive me; and also because I believe guilt to be a sterile
> disposition of the mind unlikely to further my cure. (*DL* 44)

This is dispassionate and theoretical rather than heartfelt: he clearly does
not feel Martin's absence from his life as any kind of real lack, while he
regards his marriage to Marilyn, without which Martin would not exist,
as "certainly my worst mistake" (*DL* 44).

In the following three books, the main character is childless and
expresses no desire to be otherwise. In *From the Heart of the Country*, Magda's vision of parenthood is as unappealing as her view of
marriage:

> I can imagine too falling pregnant after many moons, though
> it would not astonish me if I were barren, I look like the popu-
> lar notion of the barren woman, and then, after seven or eight
> months, giving birth to a child, with no midwife and my husband

> blind drunk in the next room, gnawing through the umbilical cord, clapping the livid babyface to my flat sour breast; and then, after a decade of closeted breeding, emerging into the light of day at the head of a litter of ratlike, runty girls, all the spit image of myself, scowling into the sun, tripping over their own feet, identically dressed in bottlegreen smocks and snubnosed black shoes. And then, after another decade of listening to their hissing and clawing, packing them off one by one to the outside world to do whatever it is that unprepossessing girls do there, live in boarding-houses and work in post-offices perhaps, and bear illegitimate ratchildren to send back to the farm for sanctuary. (HC 42)

There is no sentimental longing for motherhood here. Magda's desires are excited more by a wish for a connection with another adult—one of the servants—or her difficult father. The Magistrate in *Waiting for the Barbarians*, whatever the implications of his paternalistic relations with the barbarian girl, never expresses any regrets at his childlessness. Michael K is positively glad not to be a father:

> How fortunate that I have no children, he thought: how fortunate that I have no desire to father. I would not know what to do with a child out here in the heart of the country, who would need milk and clothes and friends and schooling. I would fail in my duties, I would be the worst of fathers. (MK 104)

Precociously clear-eyed about the position of strength that is forfeited by fathers, John, in *Boyhood*, decides that although

> he does not like Jesus…he is prepared to put up with him. At least Jesus did not pretend to be God, and died before he could become a father. That is Jesus' strength; that is how Jesus keeps his power. (B 142)

In *Youth*, he is indignant and dismayed when he finds out that he has made a girl pregnant: "In his heart he does not feel himself to be more than eight years old, ten at the most. How can a child be a father?" (Y 32). An abortion is arranged, with acquiescence but little help from him, but his thoughts keep going to what was destroyed inside her...He did not want it to live and now he does not want it to die. Yet even if he were to...save it...what would he do with it? Bring it home, keep it warm in cotton wool, try to get it to grow? How can he who is still a child bring up a child? (*Y* 35)

In *Boyhood*, he similarly rejects the notion of being a father when his mother threatens him with it:

It is a formula she uses, a formula that sounds as if it comes from the old days. Perhaps it is what each generation says to the next, as a warning, as a threat. But he does not want to hear it. "Wait until you have children." What nonsense, what a contradiction! How can a child have children? Anyway, what he would know if he were a father, if he were his own father, is precisely what he does not want to know. He will not accept the vision that she wants to force upon him: sober, disappointed, disillusioned. (*B* 162)

Tension between the points of view of children and parents is also a vital aspect of *The Master of Petersburg* and *Disgrace*. *Youth* was published after *Disgrace*, *Boyhood* immediately before it and after *The Master of Petersburg*. It is likely that the attitudes towards fatherhood expressed in the memoirs have more to do with the preoccupations of the author at the time of writing than with the actual attitudes of his younger self, given the relative absence of these preoccupations in the books written early in Coetzee's career and their importance in *The Master of Petersburg* and *Disgrace*.

Splendore contends that "the family sub-text in Coetzee's novels is rather like a buried sub-plot that is rarely allowed to surface and develop on its own terms; something the author declares 'unspeakable' and refuses to narrate" (150). But all three of Coetzee's middle-period novels explicitly concern a parent who has lost a child in some way. In *Foe*, Susan Barton comes to Cruso's island as a result of her search for her lost daughter, *Age of Iron* is addressed to Elizabeth Curren's absent daughter, *Master of Petersburg* concerns Dostoevsky's visit to St. Petersburg to find out the truth about the death of his stepson. In *Disgrace*, too, the relationship between David Lurie and his daughter is central. An element of mystery remains in *Foe* in relation to Susan Barton's daughter and the imposter Mr. Foe produces, but it is difficult to see in what way Coetzee has "refused to narrate" the family subplot in any of these novels. Moreover, children's feelings towards their parents are central to several of the novels, including *From the Heart of the Country, Life & Times of Michael K*, and *Boyhood*, and they are significant in parts of *Elizabeth Costello, Slow Man, Diary of a Bad Year*, and *Summertime*.

When Elizabeth Costello asks Paul Rayment to move to Melbourne and live with her, he suggests, "[I]s it not time you called upon your children?" She responds, "My children are far away, Paul, across the broad waves. ... I would not dream of imposing myself on my children" (*SM* 261). Not all Coetzee's parent characters are so considerate. In fact, in Costello's manifestation in the early part of *Elizabeth Costello*, she does impose herself upon her son temporarily. In lessons 3 and 4, she stays with John Bernard, her son, and his family when visiting their city to give a lecture at his college. "It is not a period he is looking forward to. His wife and his mother do not get on. It would be better were she to stay at a hotel, but he cannot bring himself to suggest that" (*EC* 59). As he fears, "hostilities are renewed almost at once" between his wife, Norma, an unemployed philosopher, and his mother, centering around Costello's evangelistic approach to vegetarianism and Norma's professional contempt for her ideas (*EC* 60). John is torn between the desire for peace and loyalty to his mother, but takes her part and comforts her distress, finally, with "There, there. It will soon be over" (*EC* 115). These two lessons and the first one, which concerns her visit to Pennsylvania with John, are all narrated through the point of the view of the son. In the rest of the book, which is focalized through her, the existence of her children is scarcely mentioned. Elizabeth Costello as a character thus never reveals from her own point of view her attitudes towards her children, either in this book or in *Slow Man*, which is consistently focalized through Paul Rayment. Given the importance of parenthood to the main characters of *Age of Iron, The Master of Petersburg*, and *Disgrace* and the lament about childlessness that runs through *Slow Man*, this seems quite a significant aberration. Costello acknowledges in her lecture that "there must be some limit to the burden of remembering that we impose on our children and grandchildren. They will have a world of their own, of which we should be less and less part" (*EC* 20). And indeed, unlike most of Coetzee's other parents, she seems content to abdicate her place in her children's lives even while she is still alive. This, perhaps, is a further indication of the fact that in *Elizabeth Costello*, dramatic realism is even less important to Coetzee than in his other novels of the period, harking back to the metafictional experiments of *From the Heart of the Country* and *Foe.*

In *Foe*, Susan Barton's child is lost to abduction. Susan travels to Brazil to search for her, and having given up, is on her way back to Europe when she is set adrift by mutineers and washes up on Cruso's island. When she recounts her story to Foe, he insists that her story should include the quest for her daughter as well as her sojourn on Cruso's island.

> We...have five parts in all: the loss of the daughter; the quest for the daughter in Brazil; abandonment of the quest, and the adventure of the island; assumption of the quest by the daughter; and reunion of the daughter with her mother. It is thus that we make up a book: loss, then quest, then recovery; beginning, then middle, then end. As to novelty, this is lent by the island episode—which is properly the second part of the middle—and by the reversal in which the daughter takes up the quest abandoned by her mother. (*F* 117)

Susan, on the other hand, says,

> [T]he story I desire to be known by is the story of the island. ... Within this larger story are inset the stories of how I came to be marooned...and of Cruso's shipwreck and early years on the island...as well as the story of Friday. ... You propose to reduce the island to an episode in the history of a woman in search of a lost daughter. (*F* 121)

The daughter who makes her appearance and claims Susan Barton as her mother is, she suspects, an impostor introduced by Foe for the purposes of his narrative. "Do you think women drop children and forget them as snakes lay eggs?" she asks him. "Only a man could entertain such a fancy" (*F* 75). Foe is clearly trespassing on Susan's rights to have her story told as she wishes, but why she wants to subordinate her narrative of parenthood to the story of the island is less easy to understand. Is the quest narrative outlined by Foe too commonplace for her liking? She tells the girl, "The world is full of stories of mothers searching for sons and daughters they gave away once, long ago. But there are no stories of daughters searching for mothers" (*F* 77). The tendency of *Foe* towards metafiction and allegory tends to make questions of realism and character motivation of little relevance, however. The real daughter is as much a pawn in the novel as the fake one, and both are less important than the power struggle between Foe and Susan and the eventual silencing of their arguments in Friday's wordless world.

Age of Iron presents itself, on the surface, as a love letter from a mother to her daughter. Elizabeth Curren seems to be a model of undemanding motherhood, writing her daughter a letter that is so self-denying that she fails to ensure that it will ever be delivered and read. However, Gilbert Yeoh argues persuasively that Mrs. Curren is an unreliable narrator, her insincerity "being masked by the seductive eloquence of her narrative" (118). Her assumptions about Vercueil's drinking and thieving, he points out, arise from baseless prejudice, and

> she infantilises the other characters, sentimentally constructing them as needy persons obligated to her largesse. It also patronizes them as ignorant persons in need of her maternal counsel and wisdom. Her discourse of maternal love, benevolence and solicitude enables a subtle subjugation of others and a reinforcement of her centrality, and is finally self-serving rather than truly loving. (123)

Even her love for her daughter is expressed in self-serving terms: "Her child rhetoric betrays her inability to love her daughter in her own right, in terms of her daughter's true otherness to her, as opposed to her daughter as a mirror of herself" (Yeoh 129). This interpretation seems to be confirmed by the rather startling passage when she repudiates her daughter's children: "They are not my grandchildren. They are too distant to be children of mine of whatever sort" (*AI* 195). What kind of mother cannot make the imaginative leap to love the children of the daughter she claims to love more than anyone else? This refusal to share the maternal feelings of her daughter denies her the equality of adulthood. A child cannot have children, her daughter is still a child in her eyes, therefore these two boys "are not my grandchildren." The context of this statement is an assertion of the superiority of the grim South African world she is living in to the safe American world where her child and grandchildren live:

> Perhaps it dispirits me that your children will never drown. ... [I]f by some mischance they ever tip out of their canoe, they will bob safely in the water, supported by their bright orange wings, till a motorboat comes to pick them up and bear them off and all is well again. ...
>   By no means do I wish death upon them. The two boys whose lives have brushed mine are in any event already dead. No, I wish your children life. But the wings you have tied on them will not guarantee them life. Life is dust between the toes. Life is dust between the teeth. Life is biting the dust. (*AI* 195)

The conclusion she reaches here negates her point. Life is denied when risk is removed, she is saying: "Life is dust between the toes." But then, carried away with her rhetoric, she says, "Life is biting the dust"; in other words, life equals death. Bheki and John are dead, killed by the very dangers of life in South Africa that she is recommending as life-enhancing, unable to be saved by her maternal intervention. In this bitter passage, Curren seems to be lashing out in envy against her daughter for being a successful parent who can protect her children, and in jealousy against those children who, unlike her, are the object of her daughter's loving care. Similarly, she says, "I cannot imagine children of his [Vercueil]," and likens him to "a boy who does not know how to love" (*AI* 196). In both cases, these attitudes show more about Curren than they do about her daughter or Vercueil: her inability to accept their parenthood, real or potential; her assumption that they are both still childish in their inability to care properly for children—in her daughter's case, paradoxically, by protecting them too well—or to reciprocate adult love. Supposing her daughter does receive this letter, how would it be for her to read these bitter, envious thoughts about her presumably beloved children, written in her mother's final days? This letter, then, becomes a monstrous imposition from beyond the grave, heartless and irrational.

And yet, it is difficult to believe that Elizabeth Curren is an entirely unreliable narrator. Yeoh's argument is seductive, but the passion of the writing in *Age of Iron* undermines its reasonableness, and Yeoh's analysis of Curren's rhetoric cannot account for a residue of pure, strong emotion rising from the page. *Age of Iron* was written in the shadow of personal bereavement and is dedicated to Coetzee's mother, father, and son, all of whom had died shortly before or during the writing of this novel. In this novel, as much as his others, as James Wood says, "Coetzee seems compelled to test his celebrated restraint against subjects and ideas whose extremity challenges novelistic representation. The excessiveness of witnessed cruelty produces a corresponding excess of shame" ("Squall Lines" 140).

In *Master of Petersburg*, Fyodor travels to St. Petersburg to seek the truth about his stepson's death. In his agony and guilt, he broods over Pavel's death. He makes an outlandish exhibition of grief at Pavel's grave:

> Unbuttoning his coat, unbuttoning his jacket, he kneels, then pitches awkwardly forward till he lies flat upon the mound, his arms extended over his head. He is crying freely, his nose is streaming. He rubs his face in the wet earth, burrows his face into it.
> …The child, to whom he has paid no attention, stares with wondering eyes. … What a Jewish performance! He thinks. But let her see! (*MP* 9)

He ignores the sensible Anna Sergeyevna's suggestions that his grief might be excessive and self-indulgent, even suggesting that she bear him a child:

> "What nonsense! You have a wife and child already!"
> "They are of a different family. You are of Pavel's family. I am of Pavel's family too." (*MP* 224)

But Pavel, as he has explained earlier, did not regard him as a father: "Pavel and I first laid eyes on each other in Semipalatinsk when he was already seven years old. … He did not take to me" (*MP* 143). The whole of this novel seems to be pulling away from Fyodor's insistent assertion of his role as Pavel's father. It is clear that Pavel was not a satisfactory son in life, that the relationship between them was strained, and that his death has left Fyodor with a huge freight of guilt, mingled with a resentful and envious belittling of Pavel's real father Isaev, "a clerk, a pen-pusher" (*MP* 152): "I am here and father Isaev is not. If, drowning, you reach for Isaev, you will grasp only a phantom hand" (*MP* 153). But Fyodor is grasping at a phantom son in Pavel, who is dead and even when alive was not really his son. A huge but almost invisible irony at the heart of this novel is his inattention to his living child, left behind in Dresden:

> The file on Pavel is closed. There is nothing to keep him in Petersburg. The train leaves at eight o'clock; by Tuesday he can be with his wife and child in Dresden. But as the hour approaches it becomes more and more inconceivable that he will remove the pictures from the shrine, blow out the candle, and give up Pavel's room to a stranger. (*MP* 154)

Reading Fyodor's narrative against the grain, in the light of this denial of the real parental bond in pursuit of the phantom, *Master of Petersburg* can be seen as a failure of parental love in the same vein as *Age of Iron*. After his exhibition at Pavel's grave, he feels "a terrible malice…toward the living, and most of all toward living children. If there were a newborn babe here at this moment, he would pluck it from its mother's arms and dash it against a rock" (*MP* 9). This is a particularly chilling statement if one thinks of his young child left with his wife in Dresden. It is clearly important to examine the sincerity of Coetzee's characters when they make exaggerated claims about their love for their children. David Lurie in *Disgrace* loves his daughter: "From the day his daughter was born he has felt for her nothing but the most spontaneous, most unstinting love" (*D* 76). He is tormented by his inability to protect her from the attack of the rapists, who lock him in the toilet and set him on fire. But when he discovers she is pregnant from the attack, it is the thought that he is "a father without the sense to have a son" that finally reduces him to tears (*D* 199). There are several suggestions that he sees Melanie as a daughter—"Almost he says, 'tell Daddy what is wrong'" (*D* 27); "[w]hen they laugh at Melanie's lines he cannot resist a flush of pride. *Mine!* He would like to say, turning to them, as if she were his daughter" (*D* 191). Lucy is clearly an independent adult from beginning—addressing him by his Christian name rather than a more affectionate relational term like "Dad" or even "Father," and after the attack, she rejects his attempts at fathering: "I cannot be a child for ever. You cannot be a father for ever" (*D* 161). Lurie, like Elizabeth Curren, has not made the transition from parent of a child to parent of an adult, and despite his protestations of love for his daughter, regrets that she is not a son and seeks to replace her with Melanie, young, beautiful, and devoid of the wit that "he has always been drawn to" in women (*D* 78); in other words, he has ceased to look for women who are his intellectual equals and is seeking a substitute child. Splendore claims that Lucy, and Magda in *From the Heart of the Country*, "two 'unlikely' mothers, recuperate a 'maternal' function towards their fathers" (159). This seems an implausible interpretation of Magda's role in her father's life, even if the murder she describes committing twice has not in fact taken place and she is still nursing him in extreme old age at the end of the novel. With Lucy, it is even less tenable. Lucy sometimes treats her father like a child, but at the end of the novel, they make their peace on the basis of equal adults:

> "Will you come in and have some tea?"
>   She makes the offer as if he were a visitor. Good. Visitorship, visitation: a new footing, a new start. (*D* 218)

The changes in David that Splendore attributes to Lucy—teaching him "to acknowledge difference and to respect the other, even a dying dog" come from his association with Bev Shaw rather than with Lucy (159). Lucy asserts their separateness, and it is on that understanding that they can begin a renewed relationship. Splendore's claim that "Coetzee's emphasis on *the idea of parents* expresses...the need to accept one's responsibilities towards the other, to behave towards the other, any other, as family" is inherently flawed when we contemplate the pathologies and distortions of feeling that seem naturally to arise between family members in Coetzee's world (150). On the other hand, she says, "there will always be a conflict between parents and children because that is the way history moves on" (150). The notion of the inevitability of conflict between generations is easier to relate to Coetzee's fictional world, where envy seems inevitably to surface between fathers and sons:

> Is it always like this between fathers and sons: jokes masking the intensest rivalry? And is that the true reason why he is bereft: because the ground of his life, the contest with his son, is gone, and his days are left empty? Not the People's Vengeance, but the Vengeance of the Sons: is that what underlies revolution—fathers envying their sons their women, sons scheming to rob their fathers' cashboxes? (*MP* 108)

Later, Fyodor thinks, "Poor child! The festival of the senses that would have been his inheritance stolen away from him! Lying in Pavel's bed, he cannot refrain from a quiver of dark triumph" (*MP* 135). Opposing the hotheaded revolutionary Nechaev's apocalyptic vision with a more cynical and cyclic view of politics, he asks him, "When one day you sit on the throne...and the land is full of princelings, hiding in cellars and attics plotting against you, what will you do?" (*MP* 188). He realizes with horror the possibility that Pavel was not an innocent but "Nechaev's comrade and follower" (*MP* 238):

> So he sits paralysed. Either Pavel remains within him, a child walled up in the crypt of his grief, weeping without cease, or he lets Pavel loose in all his rage against the rule of the fathers. Lets his own rage loose too, like a genie from a bottle, against the impiety and thanklessness of the sons. (*MP* 239)

One is reminded of the demon child in *Dusklands*: the Vietnam War personified as

> a thing, a child not mine, once a baby squat and yellow whelmed in the dead centre of my body, sucking my blood, growing by my waste, now, 1973, a hideous Mongol boy who stretches his limbs inside my hollow bones, gnaws my liver with his smiling teeth, voids his bilious filth into my systems, and will not go. (*DL* 39)

This child is not Eugene's, but is this kind of possession perhaps another facet of the kind of rivalry that appears in *Master of Petersburg*? The idea of "fathers and sons: foes: foes to the death" (*MP* 239) occurs again in *Boyhood*, this time from the point of view of the son:

> Since the day his father came back from the War they have fought, in a second war which his father has stood no chance of winning because he could never have foreseen how pitiless, how tenacious his enemy would be. For seven years that war has ground on; today he has triumphed. (*B* 159–160)

But the rivalry with his father dogs him into adulthood, when his work at IBM is "turning him into a zombie. Yet he cannot give up. ... Failing would be too much like his father" (*Y* 47). His father, bankrupted by imprudence and cheating friends, is an object of contempt:

> He burns with shame that his father should be so stupid. ... He seethes with rage all the time. *That man*, he calls his father when he speaks to his mother, too full of hatred to give him a name. (*B* 154, 156)

In *Summertime*, set in the early 1970s, John is living with his father, his mother having died (though the real Vera Coetzee died in the 1980s). Though Coetzee married in 1963 and had two children, they do not feature in the book. When Julia asks about his family, he says they have "flown... No wife, no children. I am back to being a son" (*S* 31). She doesn't ask him to elaborate. He tells his neighbor, when asked if he has children, "I am a child. I mean, I live with my father" (*S* 14). He clearly feels trapped by his father's need of him. In Margot's interview, there is a discussion of John's buying a house for his father in an isolated country town near the farm in Voëlfontein: "My father and I can't live together indefinitely, Margie," he tells her. "It makes us too miserable, both of us. It's unnatural. Fathers and sons were never meant to share a house" (*S* 133). She has, however, been struck by "the way in which he and his father behave toward each other: if not with affection, that would be saying too much, then at least with respect. The pair used to be the worst of enemies" (*S* 130). Julia feels that "John did not love his father, he did not love anybody, he was not built for love. But he did feel guilty about his father. He felt guilty and therefore behaved dutifully. With certain lapses" (*S* 48). He writes in his notebooks that he wants to be a good son, but does not know how: "If he could solve the mystery of what in the world his father wants, he might perhaps be a better son" (*S* 247). The book ends inconclusively with the choice John faces, between devoting his life to nursing his father and abandoning him: "One or the other: there is no third way" (*S* 266). J. M. Coetzee reviewed Doris Lessing's autobiography, *Under My Skin*, and remarked that "there is something depressing in the spectacle of a woman in her seventies still wrestling with an unsubjugated ghost [of her mother] from the past" ("Heart" 54). One might say something similar about Coetzee's preoccupation with his father in *Summertime*. The notebook entries which bracket the book, beginning and end, are haunted by the relationship between them, their differences in temperament, the shame he feels at the memory of destroying his father's favorite record years earlier, and the failure of his attempt to make amends. Jack Coetzee is somewhat of a cipher in the book, though Julia does detect in him on one occasion

> the tone of a parent eager to boast about his child. My heart went out to the poor man. A son in his thirties, and nothing to be said for him but that he could lay concrete! And how hard for the son too, the pressure of that longing in the parent, the longing to be proud! (*S* 41–42)

Perhaps in *Summertime*, one can detect an impulse to atone for the really quite savage attack on his father in *Boyhood*, although of course it was quite explicitly the irrational child's point of view that was represented in the earlier book. Margot offers an explanation for Jack Coetzee's weak, ineffectual nature: his father was a

> go-getter…a man with plenty of…spunk, more spunk probably than all his children put together. But perhaps that is the fate of the children of strong fathers: to be left with less than a full share of spunk. (*S* 106)

The aging J. C., in *Diary of a Bad Year*, recalls his father as

> a man who asked for little from life and received little, one who, not industrious by nature—*easygoing* might be the kindest word—nevertheless resigned himself from his middle years to a round of dull toil with little variety. One of the generation whom apartheid was designed to protect and benefit; yet how slight was his gain from it! It would take a hard heart indeed, on the Day of Judgment, to consign him to the pit of hell reserved for slavedrivers and exploiters.
> …Here he is reduced to this pitiful little box of keepsakes: and here am I, their ageing guardian. Who will save them once I am gone? What will become of them? The thought wrings my heart. (*DBY* 134–135)

Though in *Summertime*, she is barely mentioned, in *Boyhood* and *Youth*, the young John has a more complicated and ambivalent relationship with his mother than his father. His love for her is

> a fierce and angry emotion. … Should he choose (but he would never do so), he could relax into her care and for the rest of his life be borne by her. It is because he is so sure of her care that he is on his guard with her, never relaxing, never allowing her a chance. (*B* 122)

"The thought of a lifetime bowed under a debt of love baffles and infuriates him to the point where he will not kiss her, refuses to be touched by her" (*B* 47). In *Youth*, he is beginning to gain some perspective: watching the films of Satyajit Ray in London, "[i]n Apu's bitter, trapped mother, his engaging, feckless father he recognizes, with a pang of guilt, his own parents" (*Y* 93). However, he is not yet free:

> That is the trap she has built, a trap he has not yet found a way out of. If he were to cut all ties, if he were not to write at all, she would draw the worst conclusion, the worst possible; and the very thought of the grief that would pierce her at that moment makes him want to block his ears and eyes. As long as she is alive he dare not die. As long as she is alive, therefore, his life is not his own. (*Y* 99)

The carefree innocence of childhood is quite foreign to John in his daily life:

> Childhood, says the *Children's Encyclopaedia*, is a time of innocent joy, to be spent in the meadows amid buttercups and bunny-rabbits or at the hearthside absorbed in a storybook. Nothing he experiences in Worcester, at home or at school, leads him to think that childhood is anything but a time of gritting the teeth and enduring. (*B* 14)

Some of this "innocent joy," however, comes to him at Voëlfontein, his father's family farm: "Everything that is complicated in his love for his mother is uncomplicated in his love for the farm" (*B* 79). He enjoys the "slapdash mixture of English and Afrikaans" his father's family speaks; there are, at first, "all the barnyard animals of his story-books" (*B* 81), and in his cousin Agnes, he finds someone with whom he can talk about "everything, everything he did, everything he knew, everything he hoped for" (*B* 94). He feels that "no ill can happen here," on the farm (*B* 83). Even though he knows the farm will never be his, "in his secret heart he knows what the farm in its way knows too: that Voëlfontein belongs to no one. The farm is greater than any of them" (*B* 96). The farm is the one thing in his life which gives him a larger view of possibilities beyond his grim and miserable family life, though in practice, it will not provide an avenue of escape: for that, he must live through more grim, miserable years in London and, if *Summertime* is anything to go by, back in South Africa again.

Childhood, in the memories of Coetzee's other characters, is rarely simply a happy time of buttercups and bunny rabbits. Michael K spent his childhood in Huis Norensius, a children's home, and "my father was the list of rules on the door of the dormitory" (*MK* 104–105). After his mother's death, "he did not miss her, he found, except insofar as he had missed her all his life" (*MK* 34). Elizabeth Costello's son "used to think of himself as a misfortunate child, lonely and unloved," though he realizes with hindsight that he and his sister would distract themselves with singing and "would feel better, forgetting their forsakenness" (*EC* 4). Paul Rayment recalls an unhappy childhood with his Dutch stepfather, and at the thought of the Dutchman's sexual relationship with his mother, he "could explode with shame and outrage" (*SM* 241). Even Elizabeth Curren, remembering an idyllic childhood of "long sun-struck afternoons, the smell of dust under avenues of eucalyptus, the quiet rustle of water in roadside furrows, the lulling of doves," in contrast with the lives of present-day children, interprets it as "a childhood of sleep, prelude to what was meant to be a life without trouble and a smooth passage to Nirvana. Will we at least be allowed our Nirvana, we children of that bygone age? I doubt it" (*AI* 92). Given the rhetorical exaggeration she tends towards in describing her maternal feelings, it is likely that these childhood memories, used in this way to make a self-pitying point, are less than accurate.

The bond between parent and child is the first and often the most enduring bond of one's life: as Paul Rayment thinks, *"Those into whose lives you are born do not pass away. ... You bear them with you, as you hope to be borne by those who come after you"* (*SM* 8). But, for Coetzee, this bond is rarely happy and never uncomplicated, either from the perspective of the child or the parent. Happiness in such relationships occurs only in questionable memories like those of Elizabeth Curren, or in fantasies like Paul Rayment's imagined relationship with his nonexistent son, characterized by companionable father-son activities, "out for a stroll, chatting about this and that, men's talk, nothing serious" (*SM* 44), unlike anything that takes place between actual parents and children in the novels. No reassuring message of family harmony can be found in Coetzee's work.

CHAPTER 8

ENDINGS

Endings color books. Whatever shocks or delights we encounter, we reserve judgment about their significance until we have reached the end. Endings do not completely cancel previous meanings: Peter Brooks says,

> [I]f at the end of a narrative we can suspend time in a moment when past and present hold together in a metaphor…that moment does not abolish the movement, the slidings, the mistakes, and partial recognitions of the middle. (92)

Nevertheless, what characters do on the last page has a greater weight than what they do during the course of a novel.

The very fact that a fiction can end can be comforting, even if it just brings an end to the agony or discomfort of the fictional world we have been experiencing. Frank Kermode, in his seminal book on fictional endings, *The Sense of an Ending*, writes, "Tracts of time unpunctuated by meaning derived from the end are not to be borne" (162). The idea that the satisfactions of narrative depend on its finiteness is supported by the limited success of the hypertext novel. As Tim Parks says,

> If one of the challenges of narrative is not to appear contrived, but to reflect within the medium a fresh awareness of what is perceived as a meaningless and directionless world without, then the hypertext narrative is admirably equipped to do that. ...
>
> The downside of this development is that the form cannot deliver any sense of a satisfying ending. Indeed the very desirability of endings is questioned. ... There comes a point...where you begin to doubt whether tracking down what fragments may remain will add a great deal to the overall experience. At this point you appreciate that one of the most important things the standard book declares about itself, from the moment we pick it up, and then throughout our dealings with it, is its length. (207–208)

The somewhat naïve fallacy that authors of hypertext narratives seem to subscribe to is that fiction should reflect a "meaningless and directionless world without." The world unmediated is of limited interest to humans: even the most objective scientific enquiry uses narrative. The place of narrative, and of *a fortiori* narrative endings, is to tame that external world, to humanize it, to make it manageable and comprehensible. Kermode writes, "It is not that we are connoisseurs of chaos, but that we are surrounded by it, and equipped for co-existence with it only by our fictive powers" (64). Without narrative forms, it is difficult to imagine how memory would work, beyond flashes of fragmentary images. In nonliterate societies, oral tradition records history by means of storytelling. A world without narrative is a forgotten world, a world beyond history, unknowable. Brooks points out that the attempts of authors to deny us closure might make us all the more determined to construct it:

> If nothing certain is transmitted by a narrative, it may be that the reader's role in attempting the construction of what needs transmission carries the assurance of conviction. ... Narrative is one of the ways in which we speak, one of the large categories in which we think. (323)

Of course, this is not a simple process, as many theorists of narrative have observed. "We read towards 'the satisfaction of closure,'" says Patricia Howe, "a complex manoeuvre by which we construct a coherent narrative retrospectively" (138). All novelists, says Kermode, must tilt "with a hopeless chivalry against the dull windmills of a time-bound reality...but it is important that the great ones retreat from reality less perfunctorily than the authors of novelettes and detective stories" (51). Margaret Ann Doody speculates,

> Perhaps we really don't want closure—but instead, something 'to be going on with' as we say, something acknowledging the continuous life and not just artistic shape in the literary work. We meet ending, that is, only to defy it. The defiance of ending questions the justice or justness of 'meaning'. (42)

A human life is not endless and shapeless. It begins with birth and ends with death, and, as Doody points out,

> the real ending would be the death of the reader. ... We want, then, to keep that strange entity the reader alive—even at the time of departure or separation. We remind that reader of ongoing life—after weddings, after funerals, after revolution, after any historical ending. ... A novel turns to the world of becoming, and away from apocalypse. (43)

However hard the author tries to tie up all loose ends, and whatever finality might come to the characters in a novel, the reader survives and thus defies death, while at the same time mimicking death by quitting the world of the novel. It is like the satisfaction denied to George Eliot's Peter Featherstone, who, "[i]n writing the programme for his burial... certainly did not make clear to himself that his pleasure in the little drama of which it formed a part was confined to anticipation" (358). The paradoxical longing for the finality of death, at war with the survival instinct, the perfect vantage point from which we can make sense of our lives (which, of course, is only possible if we have, impossibly, survived our own death) is allayed slightly, temporarily, every time we finish a novel. As Kermode says,

> The books which seal off the long perspectives, which sever us from our losses, which represent the world of potency as a world of act, these are the books which, when the drug wears off, go on to the dump with the other empty bottles. Those that continue to interest us move through time to an end, an end we must sense even if we cannot know it. (179)

It is too much to expect that an examination of Coetzee's endings will solve the riddle of the meanings of his books. Even if his books are "about" anything, which is highly debatable, any attempt to represent these complex objects as mere ciphers to be decoded looks intolerably reductive. "Fiction allows Coetzee to pose questions without answering them. His novels withhold conclusions instead of readying them for consumption" (Szalai 85). However, it is still worthwhile to consider how his endings illuminate or complicate what has come before.

Aging and death have been persistent themes in Coetzee's work since at least *Waiting for the Barbarians*, perhaps earlier. Time after time, he brings his protagonists to the brink of death, and sometimes beyond, as in *Age of Iron* and *Summertime*. He looks to the end by creating alter egos, like Elizabeth Costello and J. C. (in *Diary of a Bad Year*), who are older than he is, and whose death is prefigured in detail within the narrative. Even David Lurie in *Disgrace* seems older than his fifty-two years, penitentially ready to resign, however reluctantly, the pleasures of life and prepare for death when he would surely be entitled to expect at least another thirty years of life.

Elleke Boehmer, in an essay about endings in South African apartheid-era novels, notes that

> [e]ven though an ending may be plural or indeterminate, even though a sense of things to come may not be completely blocked out, more often than not we encounter a reluctance to speculate or to dream, certainly to give any sort of positive reading about what might happen from now on. ... That is to say, tomorrow is

represented as struggle, or cataclysm, or the further disintegration of society. Endings are arrested in a difficult and frozen now: belief in an ongoing, unfolding destiny is largely absent. (48)

The end of apartheid did not materially change the nature of Coetzee's endings. Survival for a Coetzee character is a continuance of the pain and difficulty of existence. At best, "disabused of the fantasies devised by the mind, they arrive at a truth that is modest, humble, tethered to the ground" (Szalai 85). Certainly, as B. Kite observes, Coetzee cannot "find it in [himself] to believe in comedy's generous culminations" (17). The comedy (such as it is) of his endings is a stripped-back, absurd, and antitragical matter of dogged survival rather than the life-affirming plenitude of classic comedy on the one hand, or the cathartic satisfaction of tragedy on the other.

Dusklands, consisting as it does of two discrete narratives, has at least two endings to be considered. "The Vietnam Project" has one simple ending, one which resonates neatly with much I have proposed so far in this chapter.

> I am eager to confront life a second time, but I am not impatient to get out. There is still my entire childhood to work through before I can expect to get to the bottom of my story. My mother (whom I have not hitherto mentioned) is spreading her vampire wings for the night. My father is away being a soldier. In my cell in the heart of America, with my private toilet in the corner, I ponder and ponder. I have high hopes of finding whose fault I am. (*DL* 49)

Eugene, the psychologist, is in his element. His institutionalization has given him a temporary ending, with the luxury of withdrawing from life in order to look back at leisure and form it into a narrative, his "story," imposing the order he feels he needs, "for it is order that is going to make me well again" (*DL* 44). Of course, Eugene is deranged and barely holding together the control he so desires. He finds himself talking to his doctors "with the flashing glance and ringing tone of hysteria that even I detect" (*DL* 48). His vision of a maternal vampire hardly promises a sane and rational approach to the reconstruction of his childhood.

The overbearing mother, the absent father seem to point to a textbook diagnosis in Freudian terms, a convenient fiction. Eugene is protected by his incarceration, able to "ponder and ponder" to create his past and find out "whose fault I am." There is something touching about this wish, but it is also disturbing. Eugene's high hopes are not shared by the reader, who is likely to be skeptical about his ability to form a reasonable meaning from the raw material of his life.

The second part of *Dusklands*, "The Narrative of Jacobus Coetzee," is complicated by an afterword and an appendix. The narrative proper ends with a discussion of death:

> I too am frightened of death. I too have spent wakeful nights computing the percentage of threescore years and ten already devoured and projecting myself into the day after my decease. ...
> Yet the truer truth is that my death is merely a winter story I tell to frighten myself, to make my blankets more cosy. A world without me is inconceivable. (*DL* 106–107)

This man who has caused the death of many cannot imagine his own death. Perhaps that is a necessary precondition for murder: the conviction of one's immortality. If he could really imagine himself being "slit open" by "the undertaker's understudy" (*DL* 106), would he be able to bring himself to inflict death on another being?

But there is more:

> On the other hand, if the worst comes you will find that I am not irrevocably attached to life. I know my lessons. I too can retreat before a beckoning finger through the infinite corridors of my self. I too can attain and inhabit a point of view from which...I can be seen to be superfluous. At present I do not care to inhabit such a point of view; but when the day comes you will find that whether I am alive or dead, whether I ever lived or never was born, has never been of real concern to me. I have other things to think about. (*DL* 107)

Bravado or metafiction? "The infinite corridors of my self" recalls Eugene's investigations into his own past, the ultimate solipsism. What sort of being is not concerned about whether he is alive or dead, has ever lived or never been born? In chapter 3, I proposed a tentative solution: this is Coetzee's way of underlining Jacobus' fictional status. Questions of mortality and existence need hardly trouble a creature of the imagination. Then again, perhaps it is a final gesture of disregard for his victims, refusing to share their humanity. There is somehow a hint of aggression in the use of the second-person pronoun at just this point, coupled with the lofty assertion that "I have other things to think about."

The afterword purports to be a document written by the father of the "translator," J. M. Coetzee, S. J. Coetzee—not the real J. M. Coetzee's real father, Zacharias, an attorney, but a university lecturer—as a "work of piety toward an ancestor and one of the founders of our people" (*DL* 108). Its bogus nature is hinted in several ways, not least the Beckettian catalogue of relics left behind by the party on their journey, including ear wax, mucus, vomit, and pus (*DL* 119). The appendix, too, is spurious, though more convincing. A shorter, more matter-of-fact account of Jacobus Coetzee's 1760 expedition, "the work of a castle hack who heard out Coetzee's story with the impatience of a bureaucrat and jotted down a hasty précis for the Governor's desk" (*DL* 108), it is said to have been published in *Reizen in Zuid Afrika in de Hollandse Tijd* (The Hague, 1916), volume 1, pages 18–22. Needless to say, though this book exists, pages 18–22 do not contain this narrative. These two appendages are like steps taken back from the murderous brutality of the "Narrative of Jacobus Coetzee." Their attempted verisimilitude is at times almost jokey, perhaps detracting from the horror of the other account, but on the other hand, in their omission of any violent interracial conflict, they underline the gaps left in the literature of exploration and adventure that they parody, gaps which the "Narrative" has gruesomely filled.

Section number 266, the last section of *From the Heart of the Country*, begins, "For the present, however, it appears that nothing is going to happen" (*HC* 138). This is an anticlimax, an antiending. As Peter Strauss says, "[I]t must have been difficult for Coetzee to find an ending for

In the Heart of the Country" (121). Does this ending contain a contradictory confession? Magda asks a typical string of questions:

> Will I find the courage to die a crazy old queen in the middle
> of nowhere, unexplained by and inexplicable to the archaeolo-
> gists, her tomb full of *naïf* whitewash paintings of sky-gods; or
> am I going to yield to the spectre of reason and explain myself
> to myself in the only kind of confession we protestants know?
> (*HC* 138)

"The only kind of confession we protestants know": is that a memoir like that we have just read? Are we to assume that Magda has "yielded to the spectre of reason" and settled down to write her memoir in the manner of so many confessional autobiographers, this ending being the beginning of the writing? It seems unlikely; the book we have just read is not written from a retrospective point of view but is a monologue of someone who is making herself up in her own words as she goes along: "I have always felt easier spinning my answers out of my own bowels" (*HC* 138). No: Magda has resisted the temptation of confessing in writing, whether in memoir, sonnets, poems, or "hymns I could have written but did not because (I thought) it was too easy" (*HC* 139). These non-written hymns echo through the space of the "petrified garden, behind locked gates, near my father's bones," where she will die. But she has "uttered my life in my own voice throughout (what a consolation that is)" (*HC* 139). The hymns are unwritten, but are they not perhaps uttered nonetheless, not simply echoing soundlessly? This last passage is nostalgic and, as Strauss points out, idyllic: "I am corrupted to the bone with the beauty of this forsaken world," a "paradise" to which she had hoped to lure the sky-gods (*HC* 139). But, nevertheless, she is eager for the end, though resigned to the fact "that I may have long to wait before it is time to creep into my mausoleum and pull the door shut behind me" (*HC* 138). But the book will end: "here they come, how sweet the closing plangencies" in which she can foresee her "own destiny, which is to die here in the petrified garden" (*HC* 139). She survives the end of the book. She could achieve the retrospective narration of her life, like

Eugene in his cell, during the long wait for the moment when she can "drift into a sleep in which there are finally no voices teasing or berating. At moments like the present, filled with lugubrious thoughts, one is tempted to add up one's reckoning, tie up the loose ends" (*HC* 138). But Magda chooses not to tie up the loose ends, to explain herself to herself—or to the reader. Despite the "closing plangencies," the ending remains inconclusive.

Waiting for the Barbarians ends inconclusively as well. The Magistrate also fails to write. He tries but finds that what he has written is "devious…equivocal…reprehensible," and that "of all the people of this town I am the one least fitted to write a memorial" (*WB* 154–155). He thinks, "I have lived through an eventful year, yet understand no more of it than a babe in arms. … There has been something staring me in the face, and still I do not see it" (*WB* 155). Is the reader any wiser than the Magistrate? He, unlike Eugene, has no high hopes of deciphering his past, though he predicts that the Barbarians will soon be seduced by the comforts of civilization and that archaeologists of the future (also anticipated by Magda in *From the Heart of the Country*) will be more interested in "the relics from the desert than in anything I may leave behind. And rightly so" (*WB* 155). In the last scene, children are making a snowman in the barracks yard. "Inexplicably joyful," the Magistrate approaches. The dream which has been haunting him seems to be coming true, and he anticipates clarification, perhaps, of what has been staring him in the face. But "it is not the scene I dreamed of. Like much else nowadays I leave it feeling stupid, like a man who lost his way long ago but presses along a road that may lead nowhere" (*WB* 156). As Boehmer says, it is an "ending of sorts," but "there still seems to be no hope for pain, no promise of release" (49). Although the Magistrate has lived through his torture and regained his former position in the town, there is no triumph in his survival: his world has constricted and become less explicable, or perhaps he has just given up the attempt. The poplar slips he found in the desert will not give up their message to him, and he decides "to bury them where I found them" (*WB* 155). All his intellectual efforts, all the ideas he has entertained during the course of the narrative—about sex, the Empire, the Barbarians, torture, truth—all now seem futile, the future a matter of plodding with no hope of the kind of consummation represented by arrival, and nothing to look forward to but death.

The end of *Life & Times of Michael K* is similarly inconclusive, but, as perhaps befits someone who has refused to intellectualize, who exists rather than becomes, it has a kind of hopefulness lacking in the Magistrate's projected future. Michael has never expected much from life. He has refused to tell his story:

> At least, he thought, at least I have not been clever, and come back to Sea Point full of stories…I was mute and stupid in the beginning, I will be mute and stupid at the end. There is nothing to be ashamed of in being simple. (*MK* 182)

And there is a kind of triumph in his survival.

> Perhaps the truth is that it is enough to be out of all the camps, out of all the camps at the same time. Perhaps that is enough of an achievement, for the time being. How many people are there left who are neither locked up nor standing guard at the gate? (*MK* 182)

He is excited by thinking "*the truth, the truth about me. 'I am a gardener*'" (*MK* 181) and thinks, "[I]f there was one thing I discovered out in the country, it was that there is time enough for everything" (*MK* 183). Then, despite his earlier feeling that "[h]is was always a story with a hole in it: a wrong story, always wrong" (*MK* 110) and that "his story was paltry, not worth the telling" (*MK* 176), he wonders if he has stumbled upon meaning after all:

> (Is that the moral of it all, he thought, the moral of the whole story; that there is time enough for everything? Is that how morals come, unbidden, in the course of events, when you least expect them?) (*MK* 183)

In parenthesis and in the interrogative, this nevertheless shows Michael groping towards meaning in his life. Strange that in this ruminative mood he should think of this moral as unbidden and unexpected. How can lying awake and pondering the past be described as "in the course of events?" In this respect, Michael seems to finally be becoming something: a narrator with an autobiography with a shape and a meaning.

Michael's nostalgia for the farm, "the grey thornbushes, the rocky soil, the ring of hills, the mountains purple and pink in the distance, the great still blue empty sky..." (*MK* 183) develops almost into a plan. He imagines meeting an old man, and together they would try again to follow the route he took with his mother, having learned from his mistakes—carrying plenty of seeds this time, and avoiding Stellenbosch, "which seemed to be a place of ill luck" (*MK* 183). His peroration is almost self-satisfied. Having survived thus far and escaped confinement, he is confident that he knows how to stay free and alive:

> And if the old man climbed out of the car and stretched himself (things were gathering pace now) and looked at where the pump had been that the soldiers had blown up so that nothing should be left standing, and complained, saying, "what are we going to do about water?," he, Michael K, would produce a teaspoon from his pocket, a teaspoon and a long roll of string. He would clear the rubble from the mouth of the shaft, he would bend the handle of the teaspoon in a loop and tie the string to it, he would lower it down the shaft deep into the earth, and when he brought it up there would be water in the bowl of the spoon; and in that way, he would say, one can live. (*MK* 184)

Absurd, ridiculous, impractical: but his survival so far is equally absurd and unlikely. By reducing his needs to the barest minimum, or below, he has survived. The book's epigraph is from Heraclitus:

> War is the father of all and king of all.
> Some he shows as gods, others as men.
> Some he makes slaves, and others free.

It hardly makes sense to say that Michael K has been made free by war, but he has not been made a slave: he has remained free despite war. *Life & Times of Michael K* has one of Coetzee's most optimistic endings.

Michael has resisted and is free and capable of looking forward to a better (slightly better) future. For all we know, he might be about to die. The important thing is that Coetzee finishes at just this point, on this note of subdued but palpable hope.

Foe has one of the most analyzed endings of all Coetzee's novels. Benita Parry believes that Friday, at the end of the novel, is "in that paradisal condition where sign and object are unified, and where the body, spared the traumatic insertion into language, can give utterance to things lost or never yet heard" (47). Laura Wright says that

> ultimately, it is Friday's wordless story…that emerges and devours the other narratives by displacing Susan/Coetzee's quests for meaning. … Friday's body alone lives to haunt the text, asking to be read in its own right. (66)

Sam Durrant sees the final passage as

> an allegory of what happens both when we dream and when we read. As an allegory of dreaming, it suggests that the material suffering of the other may only be accessible to us in the form of a dream, that true wakefulness, or attentiveness to other lives, may be possible only when we are dreaming. … The liminal status of the final passage, or dive, in *Foe*, which can only take place after the death of both narrator (Susan) and author (Foe), suggests that the sympathetic imagination can encounter otherness only when the narrative has become other than itself, when it has forgotten its desire to discover the other's story. And even here, in *Foe*'s impossible *hors-text*, the empathetic leap of the imagination still falls short, landing not in the consciousness of Friday but alongside his corpse. (122)

Certainly all that is there—though is Friday a corpse in this place which is his "home," where "bodies are their own signs" (*F* 157)? If he is giving utterance, if the "slow stream" which is flowing "up through his body and out upon me" is a wordless but embodied sign, then surely Friday must be living and actively emitting this sign which "beats against my eyelids, against the skin of my face" (*F* 157).

There are echoes and oddities in this final passage. "With a sigh, with barely a splash" occurs twice, with minor variations, on page 155, harking back to the beginning of the novel (where it appears both on the first page and a few pages in [*F* 5, 11]), perhaps indicating another path which might have been taken; certainly, the phrase evokes some kind of passage from one state to another, perhaps a surrender to another element. The narrator of this final section is feeling his way around an underwater shipwreck:

> I come to a bulkhead and a stairway. The door at the head of the stairway is closed; but when I put a shoulder to it and push, the wall of water yields and I can enter.
>   It is not a country bath-house. (*F* 156)

This takes us back to the beginning of part 3. Susan Barton is talking to Foe:

> But life is never as we expect it to be. I recall an author reflecting that after death we may find ourselves not among choirs of angels but in some quite ordinary place, as for instance a bath-house on a hot afternoon, with spiders dozing in the corners; at the time it will seem like any Sunday in the country; only later will it come home to us that we are in eternity. (*F* 114)

So the narrator, though it is no longer Susan narrating in part 4, is recalling something Susan has said to Foe about life after death. The narrator, therefore, might be implying—seems to be implying—that he has died and this place he has entered, with a sigh, making barely a splash, is the afterlife.

The ending of *Foe*, whatever it might *mean*, leaves the reader with an impression of the provisional nature of this fiction. A novel that depends so much on words, writing, language, storytelling, ends somewhere that "is not a place of words" (*F* 157). The other people in the book, Susan says, are "all in the same world," even her missing daughter (*F* 152), but she leaves Friday off her list. There is almost a glibness about this ending, quite uncharacteristic of Coetzee's other work. Though it does not exactly set out meanings for us—"seal off the long perspectives" (Kermode 179)—it does seem to present a very suggestive set of conclusions for our consumption.

Age of Iron also ends with the apparent death of the narrator who has been with us from the beginning of the book. Casting her rhetorical position as writer of a letter aside, she describes what is presumably her final moments:

> I slept and woke up cold: my belly, my heart, my very bones cold. The door to the balcony was open, the curtains were waving in the wind.
>
> Vercueil stood on the balcony staring out over a sea of rustling leaves. I touched his arm, his high, peaked shoulders, the bony ridge of his spine. Through chattering teeth I spoke: "What are you looking at?"
>
> He did not answer. I stood closer. A sea of shadows beneath us, and the screen of leaves shifting, rustling, like scales over the darkness.
>
> "Is it time?" I said.
>
> I got back into bed, into the tunnel between the cold sheets. The curtains parted; he came in beside me. For the first time I smelled nothing. He took me in his arms and held me with mighty force, so that the breath went out of me in a rush. From that embrace there was no warmth to be had. (*AI* 198)

Mrs. Curren has survived horrors, though as a witness rather than a participant or victim. That she is dying in her own bed seems almost like an achievement: as Coetzee says, in answer to the question "Has Thanatos vanquished Eros?",

> In the life of each of us, Thanatos of course eventually wins, and in the life of Elizabeth Curren that is what happens. But when one looks back over the book as a whole, I would hope the outcome is less certain. (Viola 7)

The death she threatened herself with—self-immolation in a burning car outside the "house of shame" in Government Avenue (*AI* 113)—she had not "gone through with," and she has drawn back from both the threatening situations she has become involved in: she leaves the scene of Bheki's death, refusing to let the people use her car, and goes home; she spends a night sleeping rough after the death of John, subjected to the indignities of the homeless, but then she again goes home. She will go so far and no further. She will make a gesture—perhaps a fairly safe gesture—and then retreat to safety. Now, however, she has come to her end, and so has the narrative. Earlier, she has written,

> As long as the trail of words continues, you know with certainty that I have not gone through with it. ... Death may indeed be the last great foe of writing, but writing is also the foe of death. (*AI* 115–116)

The words have finished, death—with Vercueil's help—has vanquished both writing and Eros, in a temporal sense, and Curren is finally safe from "the excessiveness of witnessed cruelty" and its "corresponding excess of shame" (J. Wood, "Squall Lines" 140). Perhaps for this reason, despite Coetzee's denial that he is "an angel of mercy," "if he is an angel at all" (Viola 7), we can see Vercueil in this way. Curren thinks he is an angel—"When would the time come when the jacket fell away and great wings sprouted from his shoulders?" (*AI* 160–161)—and the ending does nothing to dispel this impression. It is very difficult to resist an allegorical or symbolic reading of Vercueil, or indeed of the novel as a whole, based on this ending.

The Master of Petersburg ends with another type of death, though this is the death of the soul rather than the body. Having written his two short stories designed as "an assault upon the innocence of a child," Fyodor "can expect no forgiveness": "To corrupt a child is to force God. The device he has made arches and springs shut like a trap, a trap to catch God" (*MP* 249). He is "perhaps outside his soul. ... *I have lost my place in my soul*, he thinks" (*MP* 249). The metaphor of death strengthens towards the end: he feels "not torment but a dull absence of torment. Like a soldier shot on the battlefield, bleeding, seeing the blood, feeling no pain, wondering, Am I dead already?" (*MP* 250).

This death of the soul is an extraordinarily dramatic image for the demands of the writing life: "*They pay him lots of money for writing books*, said the child, repeating the dead child. What they failed to say was that he had to give up his soul in return" (*MP* 250). And its impact is doubled because of its position on the last page of the book. For this reason, also, it is difficult not to extrapolate this agonizing image from character to author, or at least from the character to the author's idea of the original of that character. Does a writer have to give up his soul? These stories break his writer's block: "At last the time arrives and the hand that holds the pen begins to move. But the words it forms are not words of salvation" (*MP* 241). Stavrogin's confession in the unpublished chapter of *The Possessed* reveals "a terrible, undisguised need of punishment, the need of the cross, of public chastisement."[1] The public chastisement is, however, for the good of his soul, a means of redemption, whereas in *Master of Petersburg*, Fyodor's stories are even more dangerous: they are "a trap to catch God," and "he can expect no forgiveness" (*MP* 249). With these stories, he seems to seek damnation rather than redemption.

"He has betrayed everyone; nor does he see that his betrayals could go deeper. If he ever wanted to know whether betrayal tasted more like vinegar or like gall, now is the time" (*MP* 250). Vinegar or gall: sour or bitter? The distinction is subtle but significant. Sourness seems to come from an internal source, but it is directed outwards: it is more like part of one's disposition which might have been almost chemically changed over time by circumstances. Bitterness might be a more acute reaction, perhaps to an external event, but directed inwards. It is like the difference between spite and regret. The last line of the novel reads, "Now he begins to taste it. It tastes like gall" (*MP* 250). Bitter regret, bitter remorse. It is an uncomfortable way to end an uncomfortable novel.

Comfort has, of course, never been something Coetzee is able to offer his readers, except perhaps the sort of comfort John Bernard offers his mother in *Elizabeth Costello*: "There, there, it will soon be over" (*EC* 115). Death makes its appearance at the end of nearly every Coetzee narrative, even *Boyhood*, his memoir of childhood. The death, typically, is not untimely: John's elderly Aunt Annie has died. The undertakers are dealing with the bodily remains, but John is more concerned with her literary legacy: her father's unreadable book, of which many unsold copies remain:

> From the flat where she broke her hip to the hospital to the old age home in Stikland to Woltemade no. 3 no one has given a thought to the books except perhaps Aunt Annie herself, the books that no one will ever read; and now Aunt Annie is lying in the rain waiting for someone to find the time to bury her. He alone is left to do the thinking. How will he keep them all in his head, all the books, all the people, all the stories? And if he does not remember them who will? (*B* 166)

This feeling of responsibility towards earlier generations contrasts with his needling behavior towards his own mother, refusing at first to go to the funeral with her:

> He gets enough prayers at school, he says, he does not want to hear more. He is vocal in his scorn for the tears that are going to be shed. Giving Aunt Annie a proper funeral is just a way for her relatives to make themselves feel good. She should be buried in a hole in the garden of the old-age home. It would save money.
>
> In his heart he does not mean it. But he needs to say things like this to his mother, needs to watch her face tighten in hurt and outrage. How much more must he say before she will at last round on him and tell him to be quiet? (*B* 163)

Like Fyodor "forcing God" in *Master of Petersburg*, John is trying to "force" his mother, to make her react, even though "he would rather be blind and deaf than know what she thinks of him" (*B* 162). He is not old enough yet to be genuinely afraid of death, though "he does not like to think of" it (*B* 163). Like Jacobus Coetzee, death is for him an enjoyable "winter story" (*DL* 107), but it is also another way of forcing a reaction from an uncaring world: "He is always somehow present after his death, floating above the spectacle, enjoying the grief of those who caused it and who, now that it is too late, wish he were still alive" (*B* 164). This perverse need to provoke a reaction is more than mere petulance, though it is born of frustration. "The boy is special. Aunt Annie told his mother, and

his mother in turn told him. But what kind of special? No one ever says"
(*B* 165). Despite his irritation, he seems, in the last paragraph, to be realizing that his special quality might be in "doing the thinking," in keeping
books, people, and stories in his head. Having done that, he would then,
logically, record them for the future: the task of the writer, the kind of writer
who writes not to please but to remind his readers of difficult truths.

The end of *Disgrace* may be Coetzee's most puzzling of all. David
Lurie carries the dog that has taken to him, that enjoys his company and
even his musical endeavors, to the execution table where Bev Shaw will
inject him with a lethal dose. "He can save the young dog, if he wishes,
for another week. But a time must come, it cannot be evaded" (*D* 219).
Must a time come? Why should this dog not be kept as his pet until he
dies a natural death? Is it that he, like all creatures, is mortal, and delay-
ing his death is pointless? Or is David unwilling to take on the responsibility for the life of another being?

> He opens the cage door. "Come," he says, bends, opens his arms.
> The dog wags its crippled rear, sniffs his face, licks his cheeks,
> his lips, his ears. He does nothing to stop it. "Come."
> Bearing him in his arms like a lamb, he re-enters the surgery.
> "I thought you would save him for another week," says Bev Shaw.
> "Are you giving him up?"
> "Yes, I am giving him up." (*D* 220)

"Like a lamb," a lamb to the slaughter: biblical language used to describe
Christ's sacrifice. The implication of a ritual sacrifice is obvious. A dog's
death, like the death of Kafka's Josef K, alluded to in David's earlier
exchange with Lucy (*D* 205). Lucy Graham has analyzed the ending of
Disgrace in the light of Derrida's work on sacrificial responsibility in
The Gift of Death and claims that his killing the dog is a "gift of death"
(12), linking it back to David's treatment of Melanie: "An alternative to
Lurie's earlier sacrifice of Melanie Isaacs, this final *lösung* is a sacrificial
gesture of care for another body" (9).

There are several points to consider in this kind of reading. Firstly,
there is a question of whether David's sacrifice of the dog can be seen

as in any way redemptive. The Bible story of Abraham's willingness to sacrifice Isaac is one of the obdurate symbols of blind obedience in the Judeo-Christian tradition, but it is redeemed from its full horror by the last-minute substitution of a sheep. The sacrifice of Christ by his father was not prevented, but then he was resurrected. David's dog is neither spared nor resurrected. He, like Abraham's sheep, was, of course, an animal, not a human. In the Christian tradition, animal sacrifice is not practiced. The idea of involving animals in human ethical systems is usually regarded with abhorrence, and it is hard to believe, given Coetzee's well-known sensitivity to the being of animals displayed not only in *The Lives of Animals* and *Elizabeth Costello* but also in essays such as "Meat Country," that he does not share this abhorrence.

Did David give up this dog because he valued it, and the meaning of a sacrifice depends upon the value of the object sacrificed? Or, as Rita Barnard suspects, is it a more general gesture: "In refusing to single out the special dog, Lurie is accepting, perhaps helplessly, perhaps resolutely, the claims of an infinite number of other creatures with whom he has no special connection" (222). Barnard also warns, however, that "[t]he final scene…is not one that is readily processed; and it is essential that we do not, as it were, try to beat it into convenient shape with a critical shovel" (223). It is notable that most attempts to make sense of this scene assume that David has attained some kind of redemption with this act. Since this happens on the final page, it, more than any of his previous actions, gives definition to his narrative. However, that does not necessarily mean that Coetzee has brought him to any kind of ethical endpoint. This is David's act, and despite the feeling that he has progressed, achieving "a new footing" with Lucy and an understanding with Bev Shaw, it is not necessary to believe that he, unlike most other Coetzee characters, has attained any kind of moral resting place. If he wished to give that impression, Coetzee could have omitted the final scene and finished with David's "new start" with Lucy instead. Efforts like Graham's to fit the ending into a preexisting theoretical paradigm, or even Barnard's more tentative attempts to make sense of it, inevitably smack of the critical shovel approach. The calmness and dignity, even, of David's final actions belies the confusion the reader feels and seems to require a rational explanation. The critic who seems to see this ending most clearly is Ian Hacking in his review of *The Lives of Animals*: "*Disgrace* ends with an action I cannot comprehend, and only barely feel as possible. That is where we need Coetzee, not to make us reason, yet, but to help us experience the confusion."

The last chapter of *Youth* begins happily enough, with friendly cricket games played with John's fellow programmers, intellectual pursuits "(The Ford thesis, now nearing completion, the dismantling of logic)" (*Y* 160), and a certain amount of satisfaction in his work. "Could a bachelor's life, if it has to be a bachelor's life, be any better?" (*Y* 160). But of course, there is a worm: "A year has passed since he last wrote a line of poetry. What has happened to him? Is it true that art comes only out of misery? Must he become miserable again in order to write?" (*Y* 160) Then his work takes him to the Aldermaston weapons research station, and he "has become an accomplice in the Cold War, and on the wrong side too" (*Y* 163). The moral problem he faces is not that he does not know what he should do: "He could, if he chose, do the right thing with near infallible accuracy. What gives him pause is the question of whether he can go on being a poet while doing the right thing" (*Y* 165). From here, with clear-sighted realism, John reasons himself down to the ending: "One of these days the ambulance men will call at Ganapathy's flat and bring him out on a stretcher with a sheet over his face. When they have fetched Ganapathy they might as well come and fetch him too" (*Y* 169). As I suggest in chapter 2, this ending is almost comic in its despair, given that we know that this young man is at least loosely based on the man who will become the celebrated writer J. M. Coetzee. However, in choosing to end the book here, with his imagined end, rather than on a more cheerful or celebratory note, Coetzee has perhaps also remained truer to the bleak vision of the world which has characterized his fiction. A cheery conclusion would not suit *Youth* and would sound a false note about the career ahead that, while undoubtedly characterized by artistic triumphs, could hardly have produced works of such power and intensity if it had been easy and untroubled.

Elizabeth Costello again ends, in a sense, with death, although it has an enigmatic coda. The final lesson, "At the Gate," shows Costello in a dreamlike purgatory from which she is not released before the end: although she has managed to produce a belief in something—in frogs—for her judges, she is still awaiting their decision, and she is cut down to size by the guard who asserts that "we see people like you all the time" (*EC* 225). A lesson in patience and humility for the famous author; a characteristic inconclusive Coetzee ending.

But this lesson is followed by a postscript, "Letter of Elizabeth, Lady Chandos, to Francis Bacon." This postscript builds upon Hugo von Hofmannsthal's "Letter of Lord Chandos," in which the fictional Lord Chandos writes to his friend and patron apologizing for having given up writing, because "I have lost completely the ability to think or to speak of anything coherently," and explaining that

> the language in which I might be able not only to write but to think is neither Latin nor English, neither Italian nor Spanish, but a language none of whose words is known to me, a language in which inanimate things speak to me and wherein I may one day have to justify myself before an unknown judge. (133)

Coetzee's Lady Chandos (another Elizabeth C.—she even signs her name this way) writes, "*Not Latin*, says my Philip—I copied the words—*not Latin nor English nor Spanish nor Italian will bear the words of my revelation*" (*EC* 230). The end of the sentence, the reference to the "unknown judge," is left out, but clearly, Elizabeth Costello's predicament is foreshadowed there. Lady Chandos' letter, shorter than the Hofmannsthal piece, is a plea for help, a protest against metaphor and allegory:

> All is allegory, says my Philip. Each creature is key to all other creatures. A dog sitting in a patch of sun licking itself, says he, is at one moment a dog and at the next a vessel of revelation. And perhaps he speaks the truth, perhaps in the mind of our Creator (*our Creator*, I say) where we whirl about as if in a millrace we interpenetrate and are interpenetrated by fellow creatures by the thousand. But how I ask you can I live with rats and dogs and

> beetles crawling through me day and night, drowning and gasp-
> ing, scratching at me, tugging me, urging me deeper and deeper
> into revelation—how? *We are not made for revelation*, I want to
> cry out, *nor I nor you, my Philip*, revelation that sears the eye like
> staring into the sun. (*EC* 229)

Is this what happens to a novelist, this feeling of being "interpenetrated
by fellow creatures?" Is it a protest against critics and other readers who
persist in reading novels allegorically? And what is the significance of the
date of the letter, 11 September? That date is now so heavy with meaning
that it would be difficult to accept that it is merely a coincidence, that it
is just a plausible three weeks or so after the date of Lord Chandos' letter,
dated 22 August 1603. Nevertheless, any connections between this postscript and the attack on the World Trade Center remain obscure.

At the end, Lady Chandos writes that Lord Bacon is "known above
all men to select your words and set them in place and build your judge-
ments as a mason builds a wall with bricks" (*EC* 230). This could be a
deliberate echo of the first paragraph of lesson 1, "Realism":

> There is first of all the problem of the opening, namely, how to get
> us from where we are, which is, as yet, nowhere, to the far bank.
> It is a simple bridging problem, a problem of knocking together a
> bridge. (*EC* 1)

Building bridges, building walls; building realism, building judgments.
This first section puts its narrative structure deliberately on show and
includes discussions of realism both by the narrator and by Elizabeth
Costello in her speech:

> We used to believe that when the text said, "On the table stood a
> glass of water," there was indeed a table, and a glass of water on it,
> and we had only to look in the word-mirror of the text to see them.
>   But all that has ended. The word-mirror is broken, irreparably,
> it seems. (*EC* 19)

The postscript is also concerned with a crisis of representation by language: "It is like a contagion, saying one thing always for another (*like a*

contagion, I say)" (*EC* 228). But death appears again on the last page, even though it may be a figurative death: "Drowning, we write out of our separate fates. Save us" (*EC* 230).

Whatever meaning can be wrested from this postscript, the passion and desperation of this Elizabeth C., her sensual, wordless communication with her disturbed husband, reflect back strangely on the other, more prosaic Elizabeth C. who does not trust her visions, dismisses them as "[*t*]*oo literary*. ... A curse on literature!" (*EC* 225). James Wood points out that the postscript "is a kind of prayer, a breathing chorus, that reframes the entire book," as indeed endings are prone to do ("Frog's Life" [letter]).

Elizabeth Costello is resurrected for Coetzee's next novel, *Slow Man*, and though she has a bad heart, there is no hint of death for either her or the novel's protagonist, Paul Rayment, at the end. However, there is a proposal of marriage, as is perhaps more in keeping with the comic vein of this novel. But it is as absurd a vision of marriage as could be imagined: Paul Rayment, the one-legged man, with the aging novelist, setting off around Australia in a recumbent bicycle and a bath chair. "You could teach me doggedness and I could teach you to live on nothing, or nearly nothing. They would write articles about us in the newspapers. We would become a well-loved Australian institution," says Elizabeth (*SM* 263). Earlier, when she had first broached the subject, she had said, "If you refuse, if you insist on holding to your present dilatory course, then I will show you what I am capable of, I will show you how I can spit" (*SM* 236). But these threats turn out to be empty: when he rejects her, finally, all she can say is, "'But what am I going to do without you?' She seems to be smiling, but her lips are trembling too" (*EC* 263). Paul sends her away coolly:

> "That is up to you, Elizabeth. There are plenty of fish in the ocean, so I hear. But as for me. As for now: goodbye." And he leans forward and kisses her thrice in the formal manner he was taught as a child, left right left. (*EC* 263)

An ending of sorts, but another inconclusive one. The story of Marijana seems to be concluded; he is sending Elizabeth away, but Paul remains alone, alive, rather like the Magistrate in *Waiting for the Barbarians*, with nothing much to look forward to, although unlike the Magistrate, he is living in one of the pleasantest, safest, and most prosperous cities on earth. His barbarians at the gate are nothing but what we all face: old age and, eventually, death.

Death is a nearer prospect for J. C. in *Diary of a Bad Year*. But death does not seem so grim in his case. Anya, who knows his time is near, promises to be with him at the end, to take care of things:

> All that I will promise him, and hold his hand tight and give him a kiss on the brow, a proper kiss, just to remind him of what he is leaving behind. Good night, Señor C, I will whisper in his ear: sweet dreams, and flights of angels, and all the rest. (*DBY* 178)

As I noted in chapter 3, his voice has dwindled by the end of the book from its preeminent position filling the page to the top one-third, since the middle section, previously J. C.'s own narrative, is taken up for the last thirty pages by Anya's letter to J. C., and the lower section is Anya's own narrative, and this seems to prefigure his fading away towards death.

His final essay is in praise of Dostoevsky. Why, he asks, do Ivan Karamazov's "vengeful views" of Christianity make him weep?

> The answer has nothing to do with ethics or politics, everything to do with
> rhetoric. ... Far more powerful than the substance of his argument, which is not strong, are the accents of anguish, the personal anguish of a soul unable to bear the horrors of this world. It is the voice of Ivan, as realized by Dostoevsky, not his reasoning, that sweeps me along. (*DBY* 176)

As James Wood says,

> We can hear the same note of personal anguish in Coetzee's fiction, even as that fiction insists that it is offering not a confession but only the staging of a confession. His books make all the right postmodern noises, but their energy lies in their besotted relationship to an older, Dostoyevskian tradition, in which we feel the

desperate impress of the confessing author, however recessed and veiled." ("Squall Lines")

Here, in the final essay of the book, Coetzee pays unashamed tribute to the Russian masters:

> And one is thankful to Russia too, Mother Russia, for setting before us with such indisputable certainty the standards toward which any serious novelist must toil, even if without the faintest chance of getting there: the standard of the master Tolstoy on the one hand and of the master Dostoevsky on the other. By their example one becomes a better artist; and by better I do not mean more skilful but ethically better. They annihilate one's impurer pretensions; they clear one's eyesight; they fortify one's arm. (*DBY* 177–178)

This at the top of the page; at the bottom, Anya quoting from *Hamlet*; and in between, Anya, signing off her letter:

> I know you get a lot of fan mail from admirers which you chuck away, but I am hoping this got through to you.
>   Bye
>   Anya (admirer too)

This is almost sentimental; something we have not been used to in Coetzee's work. There was some sentiment in *Slow Man*, but it was heavily undercut by irony. In a Coetzee novel, we do not expect a beautiful young woman to interest herself in an old man dying of Parkinsonism. The old and ailing have had to make do with alcoholic tramps or nosy female novelists. Her interest is not sexual; it is not as implausible as that, but although she knows he is rich, she does not seem to be a fortune hunter. J. C. accuses himself of having been "a cold man" (*DBY* 135). Perhaps this is his (or his creator's) acknowledgment that there is, after all, warmth, generosity, and kindness in the world. The need for a clear eye and a strong arm seems to imply an army of unpleasant truths to face, but perhaps there is also a more optimistic side of life that also needs to be discerned and that he might feel he has ignored.

Although *Summertime* is nominally the third in the trilogy of memoirs begun with *Boyhood* and *Youth*, in some ways, it seems to belong more with *Diary of a Bad Year*. J. C. imagines and foreshadows his own death. In *Summertime*, Coetzee writes beyond his own imagined death. In *Boyhood*, John imagines himself as "always somehow present after his death…enjoying the grief of those who…wish he were still alive" (*B* 164). But putting himself in this position, imagining his death and the things people would say about him afterwards, he has not been able to produce effusions of grief or flattering encomiums. The compliments he awards himself are scattered. Julia, despite everything, "still look[s] back on him with affection" (*S* 63). Margot has a "lingering soft spot" for him (*S* 89), which is sorely tried when she encounters him again as an adult. Adriana can say nothing in his favor and cannot understand how he could have become so important: "I know he won a big reputation later; but was he really a great writer?" (*S* 195). The best Vincent can offer in his defense is that he was "steady…dogged" (*S* 197). To Martin, he was "a perfectly adequate academic" (*S* 212) but "a misfit…a cautious soul…If he hadn't wasted so much of his life correcting students' grammar and sitting through boring meetings he might have written more, perhaps even written better" (*S* 215). Sophie says (but only in passing) that "he wrote in English, very good English" (*S* 237), but her final judgment on his work is chilly:

> In general I would say that his work lacks ambition. The control of the elements is too tight. Nowhere do you get a feeling of a writer deforming his medium in order to say what has never been said before, which is to me the mark of great writing. Too cool, too neat, I would say. Too easy. Too lacking in passion. (*S* 242)

So, the satisfaction of imagined grief and praise eludes him. A sentence on the third-last page of the book catches the eye: "It is of course a fiction, all of it" (*S* 264). This has a localized meaning, to do with his father's illness and his employers' consoling lies. But, as I have proposed in chapter 3, there is little in *Summertime* which can be trusted as fact, and this statement reverberates back through the whole book.

The end of *Summertime* leaves John faced with a stark choice between devoting himself to his father—"abandon[ing] some of his personal projects and be[ing] a nurse" (*S* 265) or abandoning his father. "One or the other: there is no third way" (*S* 266). After the more optimistic, warmer ending of *Diary of a Bad Year*, this book, set in the South Africa of the 1970s, has a typical apartheid-era ending, "arrested in a difficult and frozen now" (Boehmer 48). This image of blocked desire and ambition, combined with the drab loneliness and lovelessness of his existence portrayed throughout the book, allows for very little in the way of transcendence. But there are a few intimations of immortality. Margot recalls a childhood conversation on the farm in the Karoo:

> "Where do you want to be buried?" he asked her one day, then without waiting for her answer whispered: "I want to be buried here." "For ever?" she said, she, her child self—"Do you want to be buried for ever?" "Just till I come out again," he replied. (*S* 108)

An odd childish quirk of thought, memorable but enigmatic. John, as an adult, ponders immortality in his manual labor, the concrete slabs he is laying which might "outlast his spell on earth," and wonders why he persists in writing, "in the faint hope that people not yet born will take the trouble to decipher them" (*S* 7). The gayest moment of the book is when he presents *Dusklands* to Julia, perhaps because he momentarily feels that he has cheated death. He tells her later that he regards a book as "a gesture of refusal in the face of time. A bid for immortality" (*S* 61). She is skeptical.

> "You want people to read you after you are dead?"
> "It affords me some consolation to cling to that prospect."
> . . .
> "But why should the people of the future bother to read the book you write if it doesn't speak to them, if it doesn't help them find meaning in their lives?"
> "Perhaps they will still like to read books that are well written." (*S* 62)

Why does he not argue that his book might speak to later generations? Being "well written" seems to be the limit of the claims he is prepared to make for his work, in the same way as coolness, doggedness, steadiness are the only personal virtues he is prepared to lay claim to.

Death, or mere survival stripped of a hope for a better future, seem to haunt most Coetzee endings. They are often enigmatic, though they never jar: his novels are always shapely objects, even those that seem most unlike novels, like *Elizabeth Costello* and *Diary of a Bad Year.* James Wood notes that *Elizabeth Costello* "has a shape, rather a religious one: it inclines towards death" ("Frog's Life"), and the same could be said of most of his books: the main character does not often actually die, but there is commonly a foreshadowing of death, a deep awareness of mortality. Even so, tragedy is not his form. The survivor is, as I propose in chapter 4, in general a comic rather than a tragic figure, even if the comedy is absurd and stark and even appalling. One thinks of these isolated figures—Magda, the Magistrate, Michael K, David Lurie, Paul Rayment—gazing towards an empty future, sometimes dejected, sometimes humbled and made wiser by their experiences, sometimes, even, with a skerrick of hope. But unlike the conventional happy ending, which attempts to smooth over the hurts and misunderstandings of the narrative, Coetzee's endings more often unsettle any feelings of optimism the books may have entertained, however briefly. Only J. C. in *Diary of a Bad Year* finds consolation on his deathbed. *Diary of a Bad Year* is such an elegiac book, gives such an impression of leave-taking, that one needs to remind oneself that J. M. Coetzee is still barely seventy, still active and writing. The time has not yet come to make his oeuvre into a shapely narrative.

Principally, however, Coetzee's endings reinforce what Szalai points out: that "his novels withhold conclusions instead of readying them for consumption" (85). They do not present readers with the satisfaction of clarification of plot and meaning, but give the more profound gratification of allowing them to continue to ponder larger questions, the answers to which are beyond the reach of ideology or even rational thought.

ENDNOTE

1. "At Tihons" in Dostoyevsky, The Possessed 701.

BIBLIOGRAPHY

Attridge, Derek. "Against Allegory: *Waiting for the Barbarians, Life & Times of Michael K,* and the Question of Literary Reading." *J. M. Coetzee and the Idea of the Public Intellectual.* Ed. Jane Poyner. Athens: Ohio University Press, 2006. 63–82. Print.

————. *J. M. Coetzee and the Ethics of Reading: Literature in the Event.* Chicago: University of Chicago Press, 2004. Print.

Attwell, David. *J. M. Coetzee: South Africa and the Politics of Writing.* Berkeley: University of California Press, 1993. Print.

Barnard, Rita. "J. M. Coetzee's *Disgrace* and the South African Pastoral." *Contemporary Literature* 44.2 (Summer 2003): 199–224. Print.

Beckett, Samuel. *The Unnamable.* New York: Grove, 1958. Print.

Boehmer, Elleke. "Endings and New Beginning: South African Fiction in Transition." *Writing South Africa: Literature, Apartheid, and Democracy, 1970–1995.* Ed. Derek Attridge and Rosemary Jolly. Cambridge, UK: Cambridge University Press, 1998. 43–56. Print.

Brooks, Peter. *Reading for the Plot: Design and Intention in Narrative.* Cambridge: Harvard University Press, 1984. Print.

Buruma, Ian. "Portrait of the Artist." *New York Review of Books.* 5 Dec. 2002: 52–53. Print.

Canepari-Labib, Michela. *Old Myths, Modern Empires: Power, Language and Identity in J. M. Coetzee's Work.* Oxford: Peter Lang, 2005. Print.

Chon, Richard, "Coetzee: Too Late for Politics?" *Buffalo Arts Review* 5.1 (Spring 1987): 6. Print.

Coetzee. J. M. *Age of Iron.* New York: Random House, 1990. Print.

————. "As a Woman Grows Older." *The New York Review*. 15 Jan. 2004: 11–14. Print.

————. "Awakening." *The New York Review*. 23 Oct. 2003: 4, 6–7. Print.

————. *Boyhood*. New York: Viking, 1999. Print.

————. *Diary of a Bad Year*. Melbourne: Text Publishing, 2007. Print.

————. *Disgrace*. New York: Viking, 1999. Print.

————. *Doubling the Point*. Ed. David Attwell. Cambridge: Harvard University Press, 1992. Print.

————. *Dusklands*. New York: Penguin, 1982. Print.

————. *Elizabeth Costello*. New York: Viking, 2003. Print.

————. *Foe*. New York: Viking, 1987. Print.

————. *From the Heart of the Country*. New York: Harper and Row, 1977. Print.

————. *Giving Offense: Essays on Censorship*. Chicago: University of Chicago Press, 1996. Print.

————. "The Heart of Me." *New York Review of Books*. 22 Dec. 1994: 51–54. Print.

————. "Homage." *Threepenny Review* 53 (1993): 5–7. Print.

————. *In the Heart of the Country*. Johannesburg: Ravan, 1978. Print.

————. *Inner Workings: Literary Essays 2000–2005*. Sydney: Knopf, 2007. Print.

————. *Life & Times of Michael K*. New York: Viking, 1984. Print.

————. *The Lives of Animals*. Princeton: Princeton University Press, 1999. Print.

————. *The Master of Petersburg*. New York: Viking, 1994. Print.

————. "Meat Country." *Granta* 52 (Dec. 1995): 43–52. Print.

————. "The Novel Today." *Upstream* 6.1 (Summer 1988): 2–5. Print.

———. "Roads to Translation." *Meanjin* 64.4 (2007): 141–151. Print.

———. *Slow Man*. Sydney: Knopf, 2005. Print.

———. *Stranger Shores: Essays 1986–1999.* New York: Viking, 2001. Print.

———. *Summertime*. Sydney: Knopf, 2009. Print.

———. *Waiting for the Barbarians*. New York: Penguin, 1982. Print.

———. *Youth*. New York: Viking, 2002. Print.

Doody, Margaret Ann. "Finales, Apocalypses, Trailings-Off." *Raritan* 15.3 (1996): 24–46. Print.

Dostoyevsky, Fyodor. *The Possessed*. Trans. Constance Garnett. New York: The Modern Library, 1936. Print.

Douthwaite, John. "Coetzee's *Disgrace*: A Linguistic Analysis of the Opening Chapter." *Towards a Transcultural Future: Literature and Society in a Post-Colonial World.* Ed. Geoffrey V. Davis et al. Amsterdam: Rodopi, 2005. 41–60. Print.

———. "Melanie: Voice and Its Suppression in J. M. Coetzee's *Disgrace*." *Current Writing* 13.1 (2001): 130–162. Print.

Durrant, Sam. "J. M. Coetzee, Elizabeth Costello, and the Limits of the Sympathetic Imagination." *J. M. Coetzee and the Idea of the Public Intellectual.* Ed. Jane Poyner. Athens: Ohio University Press, 2006. 118–134. Print.

Eliot, George. *Middlemarch*. Harmondsworth: Penguin, 1965. Print.

Gordimer, Nadine. "The Idea of Gardening." *The New York Review.* 2 Feb. 1984: 3, 6. Print.

———. Preface. *Critical Perspectives on J. M. Coetzee.* Ed. Graham Huggan and Stephen Watson. Basingstoke: Macmillan, 1996. vii–xii. Print.

Graham, Lucy. "'Yes, I Am Giving Him Up': Sacrificial Responsibility and Likeness with Dogs in JM Coetzee's Recent Fiction." *Scrutiny2: Issues in English Studies in Southern Africa* 7.1 (2002): 4–15. Print.

Graham, Lucy Valerie. "Reading the Unspeakable: Rape in JM Coetzee's *Disgrace*." *Journal of Southern African Studies* 29.2 (June 2005): 4–15. Print.

Hacking, Ian. "Our Fellow Animals." *New York Review of Books* 47.11 (29 June 2000): n. pag. Web. 30 December 2007. <http://www.ny books.com/articles/29>.

Harrison, James. "Point of View and Tense in the Novels of J. M. Coetzee." *Journal of Commonwealth Literature* 30.1 (1995): 79–85. Print.

Harvey, Melinda. "Re-educating the Romantic: Sex and the Nature-poet in J. M. Coetzee's *Disgrace*." *Sydney Studies in English* 31 (2005): 94–108. Print.

Head, Dominic. "A Belief in Frogs: J. M. Coetzee's Enduring Faith in Fiction." *J. M. Coetzee and the Idea of the Public Intellectual*. Ed. Jane Poyner. Athens: Ohio University Press, 2006. 100–117. Print.

———. *The Cambridge Introduction to J. M. Coetzee*. Cambridge, UK: Cambridge University Press, 2009. Print.

Henson, Cary. "Russian Literature in South Africa: Coetzee's Reading/ Writing of Dostoevsky." American Association of Teachers of Slavic Languages and Literatures Convention, San Francisco, CA. 28 Dec. 1998. Address. (Unpublished; available online at http://www.english. uwosh.edu/henson/coetdost1.html.)

Hofmannsthal, Hugo von. "The Letter of Lord Chandos." *Selected Prose*. Trans. Mary Hottinger, Tania Stern, and James Stern. New York: Pantheon Books, 1952. 129–141. Print.

Howe, Patricia. "'A Visibly-Appointed Stopping-Place': Narrative Endings at the End of the Century." *Theodor Fontane and the European Context: Literature, Culture and Society in Prussia and Europe*. Ed. Patricia Howe and Helen Chambers. Amsterdam: Rodopi, 2001. 137–151. Print.

Huggan, Graham, and Stephen Watson, eds. *Critical Perspectives on J. M. Coetzee*. Basingstoke: Macmillan, 1996. Print.

Janes, Regina. "'Writing Without Authority': J. M. Coetzee and His Fictions." *Salmagundi* 114–115 (Spring–Summer 1997): 103–121. Print.

Kellman, Steven G. "J. M. Coetzee and Samuel Beckett: The Translingual Link." *Comparative Literature Studies* 33.2 (1996): 161–171. Print.

Kermode, Frank. *The Sense of an Ending*. New York: Oxford University Press, 1967. Print.

Kite, B. "The Limits of Empathy." *The Believer* 3.8 (Oct. 2005): 11–18. Print.

Lawlan, Rachel. "The Master of Petersburg: Confession and Double Thoughts in Coetzee and Dostoevsky." *Ariel* 29.2 (Apr. 1998): 131–157. Print.

Lenz, Adele. Letter to the author. 1 Aug. 2007. MS. E-mail.

Mayroux, Sophie. "J. M. Coetzee and Language: A Translator's View." *Commonwealth Essays and Studies* 9.1 (1986): 8–10. Print.

McCaskill, Brian. "Charting J. M. Coetzee's Middle Voice." *Contemporary Literature* 35.3 (Fall 1994): 441–475. Print.

Morphet, Tony. "Two Interviews with J. M. Coetzee, 1983 and 1987." *Triquarterly* 69 (1987): 454–464. Print.

Mullan, John. *How Novels Work*. Oxford: Oxford University Press, 2006. Print.

Murdoch, Iris. "Iris Murdoch, Informally" [interview with W. K. Rose]. *From a Tiny Corner in the House of Fiction: Conversations with Iris Murdoch*. Ed. Gillian Dooley. Columbia: University of South Carolina Press, 2003. 18–29. Print.

The Nobel Foundation. "J. M. Coetzee Biography." 2003. Web. 16 January 2010. <http://nobelprize.org/nobel_prizes/literature/laureates/2003/coetzee-bio.html>.

Parks, Tim. "Tales Told by a Computer." *The Fighter: Essays.* London: Harvill Secker, 2007. 199–213. Print.

Parry, Benita. "Speech and Silence in the Fictions of J. M. Coetzee." *Critical Perspectives on J. M. Coetzee.* Ed. Graham Huggan and Stephen Watson. Houndmills: Macmillan, 1996. 37–65. Print.

Scanlan, Margaret. "Incriminating Documents: Nechaev and Dostoevsky in J. M. Coetzee's *The Master of Petersburg.*" *Philological Quarterly* 76.4 (Fall 1997): 463–477. Print.

Scott, Joanna. "Voice and Trajectory: An Interview with J. M. Coetzee." *Salmagundi* 114/115 (1997): 82–102. Print.

Sévry, Jean. "An Interview with J. M. Coetzee." *Commonwealth Essays and Studies* 8.1 (1985): 1–7. Print.

Shlomowitz, Ralph. Letter to the author. 30 July 2007. MS. Personal communication.

Slovak, Paul. Letter to book review editor, Viking Penguin, New York. 10 June 1997. TS.

Sontag, Susan. "The Pornographic Imagination." *Styles of Radical Will.* London: Vintage, 1994. 35–73. Print.

Splendore, Paola. "'No More Mothers and Fathers': The Family as Sub-Text in J. M. Coetzee's Novels." *Journal of Commonwealth Literature* 38 (2003): 148–161. Print.

Strauss, Peter. "Coetzee's Idylls: The Ending of *In the Heart of the Country.*" *Momentum: On Recent South African Writing.* Ed. M. J. Daymond, J. U. Jacobs, and Margaret Lenta. Pietermaritzburg: University of Natal Press, 1984. 121–128. Print.

Swales, Martin. "Sex, Shame and Guilt: Reflections on Bernhard Schlink's *Der Vorleser* (*The Reader*) and J. M. Coetzee's *Disgrace.*" *Journal of European Studies* 33.1 (2003): 7–22. Print.

Szalai, Jennifer. "Harvest of a Quiet Eye," *Harper's Magazine* 309.1850 (1 July 2004): 85. Print.

Viola, André. "An Interview with J. M. Coetzee." *Commonwealth Essays and Studies* 14.2 (1992): 6–7. Print.

Wachtel, Eleanor. "The Sympathetic Imagination: A Conversation with J. M. Coetzee." *Brick* 56 (2001): 37–47. Print.

Watson, Stephen. "Speaking: J. M. Coetzee." *Speak* 1.3 (May/June 1978): 21–24. Print.

Wood, James. "Coetzee's *Disgrace*: A Few Skeptical Thoughts." *The Irresponsible Self: On Laughter and the Novel*. New York: Farrar, Straus and Giroux, 2004. 246–257. Print.

———. "A Frog's Life." *London Review of Books* 25.20 (23 Oct. 2003): n. pag. Web. 22 July 2007. <http://www.lrb.co.uk/v25/n20/wood02.html>.

———. "A Frog's Life" [Letter to the editor]. *London Review of Books* 25.23 (4 Dec. 2003): n. pag. Web. 31 December 2007. <http://www.lrb.co.uk/v25/n23/letters.html>.

———. *The Irresponsible Self: On Laughter and the Novel*. New York: Farrar, Straus and Giroux, 2004. Print.

———. "Squall Lines." *The New Yorker.* 24 Dec. 2007: 140. Print. 31 December 2007.

Wood, Philip R. "Aporias of the Postcolonial Subject: Correspondence with J. M. Coetzee." *South Atlantic Quarterly* 93.1 (Winter 1994): 181–195. Print.

Wright, Laura. "A Feminist-Vegetarian Defense of Elizabeth Costello: A Rant from an Ethical Academic on J. M. Coetzee's *The Lives of Animals*." *J. M. Coetzee and the Idea of the Public Intellectual*. Ed. Jane Poyner. Athens: Ohio University Press, 2006. 193–216. Print.

———. *Writing "Out of All the Camps": J. M. Coetzee's Narratives of Displacement*. New York: Routledge, 2006. Print.

Yeoh, Gilbert. "Love and Indifference in J. M. Coetzee's *Age of Iron*." *Journal of Commonwealth Literature* 38 (2003): 107–134. Print.

INDEX

Lightning Source UK Ltd.
Milton Keynes UK
30 December 2010

165030UK00001B/14/P